INFANT DEVELOPMENT

INFANT DEVELOPMENT

*The embryology
of early human behavior*

BY ARNOLD GESELL, M.D.

GREENWOOD PRESS, PUBLISHERS
WESTPORT, CONNECTICUT

Library of Congress Cataloging in Publication Data

Gesell, Arnold Lucius, 1880-1961.
    Infant development; the embryology of early human
behavior.

    Includes bibliographies.
    1. Developmental psychobiology. I. Title.
RJ131.G49 1972   155.4'12   73-142858
ISBN 0-8371-5957-1

Originally published in 1952
by Harper & Brothers, New York

Reprinted with the permission
of Harper & Row, Publishers

Reprinted by Greenwood Press,
a division of Williamhouse-Regency Inc.

First Greenwood Reprinting 1972
Second Greenwood Reprinting 1973
Third Greenwood Reprinting 1975

Library of Congress Catalog Card Number 73-142858

ISBN 0-8371-5957-1

Printed in the United States of America

Contents

Preface and Acknowledgments

Over a period of more than thirty-five years, the work of the former Clinic of Child Development at Yale University has been reported from time to time in the form of books, monographs, numerous papers, and a score of edited sound and silent films. Our interest in cinematography as both a research and a teaching tool, lies in the background and the foreground of the present volume.

The systematic investigations of the clinic up to the year 1948 and the child vision research from 1948 to 1950 were concerned with a charting of the growth and forms of behavior at advancing maturity levels from birth to the tenth year.* The research methods and the diagnostic and guidance service of the clinic were recorded in 1946 in a documentary film produced by *March of Time.*

More recently the writer was afforded a unique opportunity to assist in the production of a new type of film, namely, a conceptual film dealing with the principles and pediatric applications of a clinical science of child development. Further mention of this undertaking will be made in the Introduction and opening chapters which follow. A fortunate combination of circumstances and the exceptionally fine equipment of the C. L. Welsh Studio at Greenwich, Connecticut, made possible a high degree of co-operative planning by a production team of several experts in various aspects of cinematography.

The production team consisted of the following persons in consultation with Dr. David Ruhe, Director of the Medical Film Institute of the Association of American Medical Colleges and with

* These studies, normative and psychogenetic, are now being extended into the years from ten to sixteen under the auspices of the Gesell Institute of Child Development. This institute located in New Haven, Connecticut, was incorporated in 1950 by the research group of the former Yale Clinic of Child Development. The current work of the institute was documented for television broadcast in the *March of Time over the Years* series (1951). The television film incorporated the 1946 film, to show the continuity of the past with the present program of developmental research and service.

Captain Robert Schultz in charge of the Audio-Visual Section of the Bureau of Medicine and Surgery of the Department of the Navy; Mr. C. L. Welsh, producer-cameraman; V. F. Bazilauskas, M.D., medical animator; Leon Rhodes, associate animator; J. E. Maurer, sound engineer; Bernard V. Dryer, film architect; and Louise B. Ames, Ph.D., cinema research associate. The writer served as technical director of the research report and as narrator of the film.

I wish to express cordial acknowledgments to all my associates in the making of this co-operative film. Their zeal and generous identification with the objective of the film have placed us in their debt. Each had a distinctive talent to contribute. The most exacting and onerous technical tasks in color photography fell upon Mr. C. L. Welsh, and I appreciatively testify to his extraordinary meticulousness and high standards of craftsmanship.

My grateful acknowledgment goes to the parents, social workers, nurses and physicians who participated in our joint undertaking. As for the infants, they seemed to take it for granted that they had an important part to play. I must add specific mention of Dr. Joseph Henry DiLeo who is in charge of the department of developmental pediatrics at the New York Foundling Hospital and who rendered invaluable assistance in making subjects available to us.

With the completion of the conceptual film and of the systematic survey covering the first ten years of life, it seemed desirable to gather into a single, concise view the theoretical and practical implications set forth in the underlying studies. The result is this small volume, which is in no sense a formal summary but rather an informal orientational introduction.

The concealed process of growth is revealed in its products. We hope that the pictorial chapter will give a compact intimation of the organic sweep of the early life cycle. Embryology deals with the genesis and growth of organic forms, physical and functional, postnatal as well as prenatal. The patterning of infant behavior therefore falls within the scope of embryology.

The embryological forces are deeply entrenched because they are the culminations of countless ages of evolution. Growth accordingly becomes a key concept for interpreting the nature and the needs of the human action system, while it is in the making in fetus, infant, and child.

ARNOLD GESELL

Gesell Institute of Child Development
New Haven, Connecticut

The Concept of Growth

The present volume, despite its slenderness, deals with the vast concepts of growth and of embryology as they apply to the patterning of human behavior. As a division of the biology of man, the field of embryology is usually limited to the prenatal and bodily development of the organism. But Huxley rightly insisted that the science of embryology embraces the total life cycle. We shall attempt, in the following chapters, to show that there is a significant continuity in the prenatal and postnatal phases of human growth.*

This continuity comprises functional as well as physical development. Organisms behave. Their behavior characters are as distinctive as their physical characters. Growth is a patterning process which simultaneously organizes the forms of body, bones, and brain—and of behavior. We shall be particularly concerned with the forms and the genetic transformations of behavior, always mindful of the fact that the child grows as a unit. He comes by his mind, as he comes by his body, through the organizing processes of growth.

The growth of behavior can be investigated by various methods —naturalistic, normative, experimental, anthropemetric, photographic and clinical. The co-operative studies at Yale University by the staff of the former Clinic of Child Development (1911-1948) made use of the foregoing methods to chart the progressions of behavior development for the first ten years of life. Motor, language, adaptive, and personal-social behavior were included in the basic survey. A special study of the development of visual behavior was completed in the period from 1948 to 1950.

Systematic cinematography was used to record and to analyze the conformation and the developmental sequences of behavior patterns

---

* A study of the fetal and circumnatal phases of behavior development was reported by the authors in an earlier volume, illustrated by 300 action photographs. See THE EMBRYOLOGY OF BEHAVIOR: *The Beginnings of the Human Mind*, Harper & Brothers, New York, 1945; pp. 289. (By A. Gesell in collaboration with C. S. Amatruda).

of normal infants at periodic ages. These tangible and cumulative records supplied a framework of objective reality for our study of human infancy. Such concrete data do not, of course, answer all of the questions one might ask concerning the embryonic psyche; but they do permit us to view the "mind" of the infant as a structured action system, governed by deep-seated laws of growth.

Accordingly, the concept of growth becomes more than an empty abstraction to conjure with. The sequences of growth, whether plant, animal, or human, are mainfestations of the order of Nature. A recognition of the natural sequences of infant development should further a better understanding of the nature and needs of all types of children—normal, defective, and handicapped. Growth phenomena have special theoretical and practical implications for students of medicine.

These implications enlisted the initiative and interest of the recently established Medical Film Institute of the Association of American Medical Colleges. An informal committee made an investigation of the resources of the Photographic Research Library of the Yale Films of Child Development. With the active co-operation of the Bureau of Medicine and Surgery of the Department of the Navy and of the Office of Naval Research, it was decided to produce a full-length research report film interpreting the methods and findings of the Yale Clinic. Emphasis was placed upon interpretation because the Medical Film Institute and sponsors were particularly interested to demonstrate the educational advantages of a *conceptual type of motion picture* as opposed to a purely factual, or documentary, film.

To relate the field of embryology to the morphogenesis of behavior and to the developmental psychology of human abilities presented a challenge to the cinema as a medium of communication. Growth is an elusive process beyond direct observation. Can the unique semantics of the visual language of the cinema be utilized to increase an awareness of the lawful nature of early human growth?

This central question guided the construction of a feature-length conceptual film which in a year's time was produced under the title "The Embryology of Human Behavior."*

* This film, a 16mm. color version, is distributed by the International Film Bureau, 6 North Michigan Avenue, Chicago 2, Illinois and may be secured by purchase or rental arrangement. A weekly rental rate is available to schools and institutions desiring to use the film for extended periods.

The contents of the resultant film are partly reflected in the pictorial chapter (Chapter Two) of the present volume. The film combined live color photography with interpretive animation, also in color. To enhance the continuity of the growth cycle the photography and the commentary focused particularly upon the patterning of eye-hand behavior in fetus and infant. The film outlines the progressions of normal development. A concluding clinical section illustrates the technique of infant behavior examination in the developmental diagnosis of defects and deviations.

The demands of film construction have compelled us to review previous publications in an effort to clarify and to visualize the processes and manifestations of growth. The present book, like the film, aims to compress into short space some of the scientific import of familiar growth phenomena, and to go beneath the deceptive layer of obviousness which conceals the psychological and the clinical significance of infant behavior.

Book and film are quite independent of each other, but they have a common purpose: to convey a concept and to invite a relativistic outlook upon the manifold problems of child development.

The general plan of our book is evident from the table of contents. Our purpose is not to summarize a vast field, but rather to indicate the pervasive role of an intrinsic embryology in the morphogenesis of the human action system. We shall, for conciseness, cleave closely to the central concept. It is not, of course, assumed that growth takes place in a vacuum. Growth always occurs in a milieu and is configured by factors which support it. In growth or development (the terms are interchangeable) the mutual fitness of organism and environment is brought to progressive realization.

It is futile to separate sharply the innate and the extrinsic aspects. The organism grows as a unit, and growth is itself a unifying process. But it is also a creative one. The so-called environment (extrinsic factors) cannot generate the progressions of ontogenesis—the momentous movement from zygote to embryo to fetus to infant, and the dramatic advance from limb bud to hand to reflex grasp to voluntary prehension, manipulation, and construction.

These progressions are primarily governed by genes functioning as chemical agents obedient to cues. Maturational mechanisms underlie the marvelous sequences of ontogenesis. Maturation is the net sum of the gene effects operating in a self-limited life cycle.

It is this inherent embryology which invites our attention.

INFANT DEVELOPMENT

CHAPTER ONE

Charting the Normal Growth Cycle

Cinema Studies of the Patterning of Behavior

How did we become interested in charting the early stages of human growth? And what led us to adopt the cinema as a fundamental tool of research? The two questions are not unrelated. No age of childhood can be understood without some knowledge of the adjacent ages—the ages which precede and which follow. In infancy the transformations from age to age are so bewilderingly complex that observation and memory need the support of photography. The cinema, as we shall indicate, proved essential for an objective approach to the psychology of early growth.

The Yale Clinic of Child Development was established (in 1911) as one of the service clinics of the New Haven Dispensary, affiliated with the school of medicine. At the outset the work of the clinic was largely limited to the mental diagnosis of backward, defective, and delinquent children of adolescent and school ages. But very soon our interest shifted to earlier age levels. We began to ask ourselves what were these problem children like in their preschool years. When did they first show the symptoms which finally brought them to the clinic? From the standpoint of preventive medicine, was it not desirable to identify defects and deviations of development at the earliest possible age?

There were other questions to ask: How early can a mental diagnosis be made? Is it feasible to measure a baby's intelligence? What is the nature of the infant mind? Are babies born alike and is it possible to estimate the influence of environment? And how can one "get at" a baby's mentality? An infant cannot introspect and talk with you. He cannot attend to quiz questions such as we were routinely using with older children—"Is it morning or afternoon?" "Are you a boy or a girl?" "What is the difference between wood and glass?" If a baby could only talk, how much simpler it would be to conduct a mental examination!

Yet we could not go on the premise that all mental diagnosis must be deferred until a child reaches the age of verbal comprehension and speaks in sentences. From the standpoint of preventive medicine, we inclined to the belief that the infant from the beginning has a mind which makes itself manifest in accessible signs and symptoms. Fortunately our clinic at the dispensary was located within earshot of a busy Well-Baby Conference. We simply had to step across a narrow hallway to look upon normal infants in all their intriguing variety at every stage of their fast-moving development. It was easy to persuade the mothers to bring their babies into our own examining room.

Did the babies co-operate? They always do, in the sense that they frankly display patterns of behavior which indicate their stage of development. Behavior is the baby's language. He "tells" us a great deal in his actions even though he may lack words.

The first observations of our young visitors from across the hall were quite informal and naturalistic. We simply watched the baby's spontaneous behavior while he sat in his mother's lap, noting his postures, his regard for surroundings, his reference to his mother, his facial expressions, and his self-prompted playful activities. Presently we moved a small adjustable table into the scene of observation. Still safe in the security of his mother's lap, the baby confronted the table, which now became a test table, on which we placed selected test objects to elicit behavior responses. A red one-inch cube was placed within easy reach. At once the baby began to tell us the state of his "mind" by the manner in which he used his eyes and hands in reaction to the cube. Did he merely look at the cube? How steadily did he hold his head and his ocular fixation? Did he bring this hand to the table top? Did he corral the cube with two hands or reach out with one? Did he grasp with his palm or with finger tips? Did he oppose his thumb? Did he bang the cube? Did he give heed to a second cube? Did he pick up the second and did he combine the two cubes? These questions and many others were answered in the baby's language, namely in distinctive forms of behavior.

Each baby reacted with behavior patterns characteristic of his individuality and of his stage of maturity. We varied our test situations to secure further evidence of the underlying patterning processes. We presented single cubes in succession; we presented ten cubes in mass formation; a string to pull, attached to a ring; a cup and spoon to combine; a pellet to pluck. These test situations revealed much concerning the infant's eye-hand co-ordination. Other situations threw light on posture and locomotion, on his ability to solve simple problems (like placing a cube into a cup), his capacity to imitate, his vocalizations, his reactions to persons, and so on.

With cumulative observations it became increasingly interesting to compare the behavior traits of one age level with those of another. For example at six months of age the infant reacted to a tiny sugar pellet (7 mm. in diameter) by a crude ineffectual raking response. At nine months he could pluck the pellet rather deftly, using index finger and thumb as forceps. In spite of a rich range of individual variations it became apparent that there is a basic ground plan of development consistent with advancing levels of maturity. The individual differences could be interpreted as variants of this ground plan.

Our objective approach to the study of the infant led in due course to certain conclusions:

(a) The infant has a mind.

(b) The infant comes by his mind as he comes by his body, that is, through the organizing processes of growth.

(c) He develops as a unitary action system.

(d) This action system is manifested in patterns of behavior which are governed by deep-seated (ontogenetic) laws of developmental sequence.

(e) Graded functional tests of behavior can therefore be utilized to determine the maturity of the growing action system and the integrity of the underlying nervous system.

To devise appropriate behavior tests and to arrange the multifarious behavior traits into growth sequences entailed an extensive program of research. The results of this systematic research are reported in several volumes listed elsewhere. Working as a co-operative group of investigators, the staff of the Yale Clinic of Child Development charted behavior traits characteristic of thirty-four advancing levels of maturity from birth to ten years of age. All told, some three thousand behavior items were finally available for classification into growth gradients and normative developmental schedules. The basic survey was concerned with normal mental growth; but the methods of behavior examination and the findings were constantly put to test on the diagnostic service for backward, defective, and deviant children.

Primary attention was given to the first five years of life. A special study of the behavior characteristics of a series of fetal-infants (premature infants) threw light on growth changes which ordinarily take place in the prenatal period. The basic research group of normal (full-term) infants were studied at lunar-month intervals by means of standardized behavior examinations, by naturalistic observations of spontaneous and incidental behavior, by home visits and parental interviews. The developmental data comprised four major fields of behavior: motor, adaptive, language, and personal-social.

The study of infant behavior in its wealth of transformations is comparable to the task of developmental anatomy. Behavior, as it grows, assumes forms. The forms in their inherent organization manifest the anatomy, the morphology, and the embryology of the action system.

Fortunately we have at our disposal a powerful instrument for recording these forms in their multitudinous detail, namely, the cinema. Taking a hint from astronomy, the clinic contrived a photographic observation dome, equipped with cameras mounted on two quadrants. The cameras, however, did not point to the heavens; they were directed inward to a central universal focal area occupied by the infant, who put forth his appropriate patterns of behavior for the record.

At first the cinema records were limited to the progressions of normal infant development, but from time to time significant clinical deviations were similarly documented. Later a parallel naturalistic survey recorded the infant's daily life in domestic surroundings under the mother's immediate care—his sleep, feeding, bath, play, bodily activities, and social behavior. The normative and the naturalistic surveys provided the source material for *An Atlas of Infant Behavior*: A Systematic Delineation of the Forms and Early Growth of Human Behavior Patterns. This work in two volumes was illustrated with 3,200 action photographs. The normative series depicted typical trends from age to age. The naturalistic series portrayed individual differences.

The scientific value of cinematography as a research tool rests upon three paradoxes: (1) The cinema captures motion by stilling it. (2) The cinema embalms the behavior (the motion) in a chemical emulsion, yet reanimates it in its original living integrity. (3) It converts past and future into a present.

Cinemanalysis is a research technique which capitalizes these three paradoxes, and uses the almost magical time-space manipulability of the flexible film to explore the patterns of behavior in relation to spatial form and temporal sequences. The simplest device for accomplishing cinemanalysis is a vertically mounted, portable projector, operated by a hand crank, to throw a 4 by 5-inch image on a screen for close, intimate inspection.

By controlling the crank the student comes into intimate grips with the behavior record. It may be a normative record which depicts normal patterns of eye-hand co-ordination typical of a given age level. It may be a clinical record of a cerebral injury which shows the distortion of patterns caused by a neurological lesion. The student stills, starts, slows, speeds, and reviews the successive images to suit his interest and purpose. He employs the analytic viewer in much the same way that he would use a microscope for histological observation. When any given behavior pattern is once captured by the film, it becomes as tangible as tissue for the inquiring observer. Indeed, there is another analogy and a corollary. Just as histology serves the study of the embryology of tissues and organs, so cinemanalysis can serve the study of the embryology of behavior.

The cinema registers not only the moments and the passing episodes of behavior. It also records the far-reaching progressions from age to age—the epochs and the cycle of growth. To see these transformations in their lawful unfoldment is to realize that the infant mind is a living, organized reality, which has a dynamic morphology shaped by deep-seated mechanisms of growth.

CHAPTER TWO

The Embryology of Human Behavior

A Visualization of the Cycle of Growth

The title of this chapter is also the title of the conceptual film which was described in the preceding pages. This pictorial chapter assembles some fifty cinephotographs from the original film and arranges them in sequence with the narrative script of the spoken commentary. The narration is reproduced in its entirety. The photographs have been selected to enable the reader to sense in rapid sweep the progressions of the growth cycle. Although static instantaneous photographs cannot impart the dynamic flow of a motion picture, they make it possible to visualize the lines, the directions, and the resultant patterns of the growth complex. The series of photographs here reproduced may serve as points of departure for mobilizing the reader's own imagery. The text of the running story appears on the adjoining (left-hand) pages. The portions of the narration which refer specifically to the selected illustrations are italicized. Approximate chronological ages of the growth cycle are designated.

No one has actually seen in their subtlety the continuous movements of the growth process. The power and the designs of these movements must be inferred from the ever-changing products of growth. Inasmuch as the child develops as an indivisible unit, the products assume both physical and functional forms. Body and mind grow concomitantly. As the soma takes shape, the psyche likewise takes shape in the depths which are beyond immediate observation. Irrespective of all metaphysical considerations, the growing infant may be visualized as a growing action system. The following pages, in outline, portray this action system in its early, fundamental making.

Growth Cycle   Age: 4 weeks

Even while a child sleeps, he grows.
He develops as an individual, but he obeys laws of growth which
are universal.

He comes by his behavior as he comes by his body.
He develops the capacity to wake up spontaneously.

He stirs.
His eyes open to receive light.

His hands are mostly closed, but brain, hands, and eyes are coming
into increasing co-ordination.

Behavior patterns are forming.

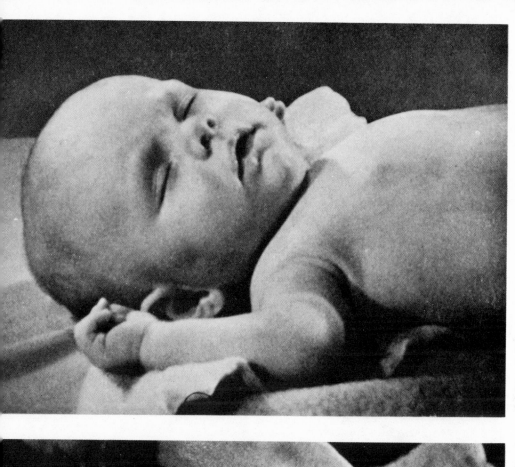

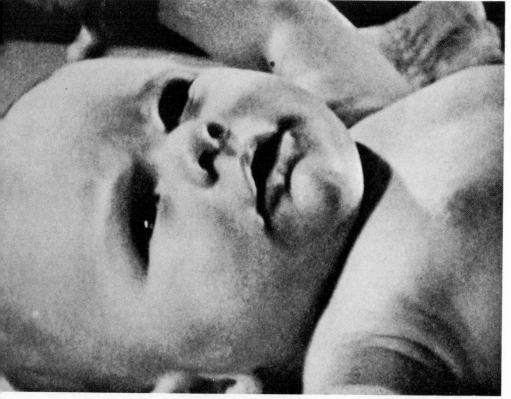

Growth Cycle   Fetal Age: 8 weeks

The patterning process began long before the infant was born—even in the darkness of the uterus.

In the embryo, one lunar month after conception, brain, eyes, and hands are already taking form.

The heart soon begins its rhythmic lifelong beat.

The retina develops as an outgrowth of the brain.

The rudimentary hands likewise are coming into linkage with the nervous system.

In 2 months the embryo becomes a fetus.

The fetus is capable of small, almost imperceptible movements— flexor movements of trunk and shoulders.

In another month the neuromuscular organization penetrates to forearm and fingers.

The fetus at five months foreshadows the infant of the future: his body conformation becomes individual.

A vast network of nerves—countless sensory and motor neurons and connecting circuits have brought into being a total action system. This action system includes five hundred pairs of skeletal muscles which activate trunk, limbs, hands, face, mouth, and eyes.

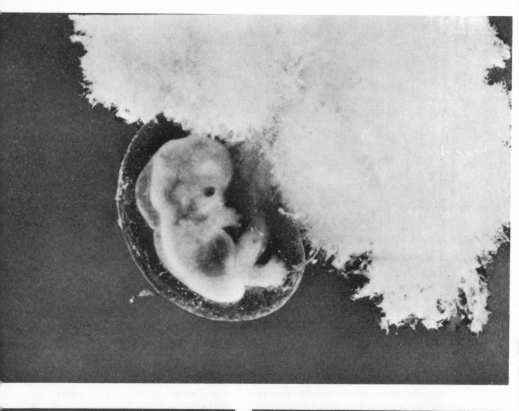

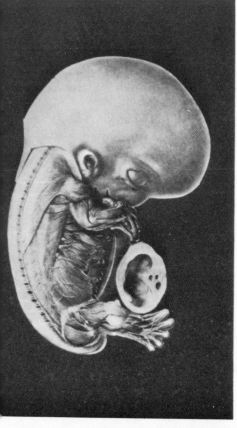

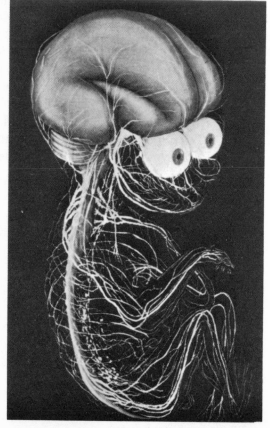

The eyes are motor as well as sensory organs, coming into increased connection with the cortex.
At the fifth prenatal month each eye moves independently, activated by its own oculomotor muscles and motor neurons.
These early eye movements are sketchy, fitful, and variable.

Inside the developing eye the receptor neurons of the retina have meanwhile differentiated into distinctive microscopic layers, exquisitely intricate.

Inside the brain the neurons of the optic cortex and subcortex, immature neurons elaborate with their dendrites, axons, and collaterals. Vision is in the making.

By the seventh prenatal month a continuous neuron connection is established between the cortex and a more highly differentiated retina.
The visual path is complete and capable of functioning.
Brain, retina, and oculomotor muscles have been linked.
The eyes may move co-ordinately even in the uterus.

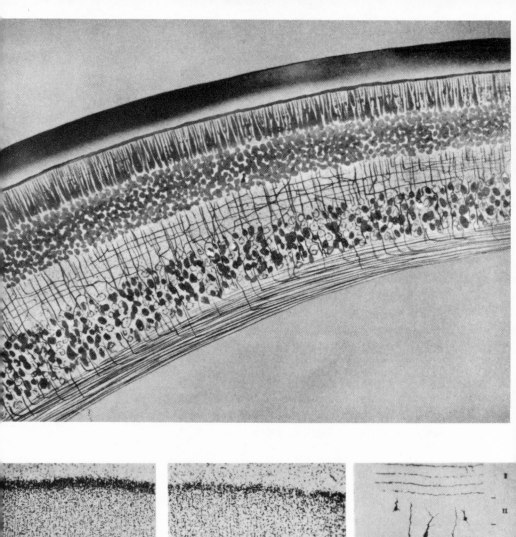
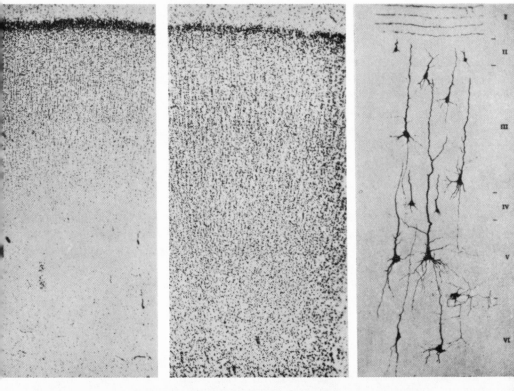

In the newborn infant the eyes begin to move as though seeking experience.
They rove, but tend to look in the sidewise direction of the averted head.

The month-old infant assumes a well-defined asymmetric posture, the tonic-neck-reflex posture, a kind of fencing attitude—head to one side, one arm extended, the other flexed toward the shoulder. This behavior pattern—here in stop motion—channelizes vision toward the outstretched hand—a reflex attitude so basic that it is already present in the fetal infant, born two months prematurely.

The asymmetric tonic-neck posture dominates the action system, either in right- or left-hand versions.

Handedness is in the making.
At the age of 2 months the infant's eyes are more mobile. They seek distant light areas and may ignore the ring dangled in the near field of vision.

The ring moves across the field, but he does not at present pursue it either with eyes or hands.

By the age of three months he shows more visual interest in nearby objects. Spontaneously he looks at his own hands—an important forward step in the embryology of eye-hand behavior.
His eyes now fix upon the dangling ring. They pursue it in the rightward quadrant—to the midline.
But the right tonic orientation prevents them from following through.

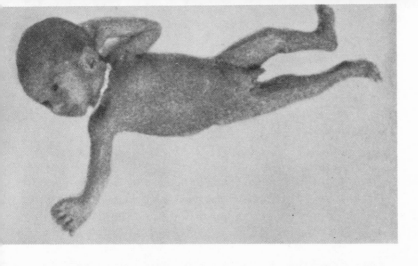

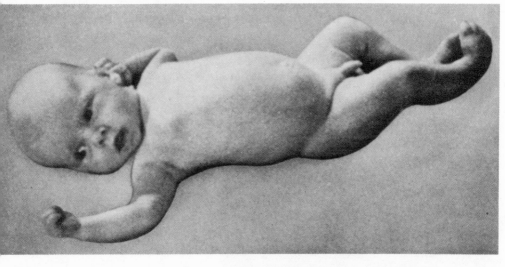

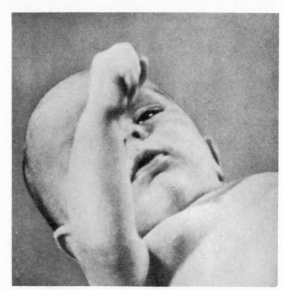

Growth Cycle   Ages: 4 months and 5 months

At about four months, however, both head and hands begin to prefer the midplane. Asymmetric postures give way to symmetric postures. The eyes now converge and fasten upon the dangling ring at midpoint.

At about five months, the eyes pursue the dangling ring with greater competence, both rightward and leftward.
The hands now close in upon the ring: primitive prehension has been achieved.

The eyes are pathfinders.
The infant takes hold of the world with his eyes long before he takes hold with his hands.

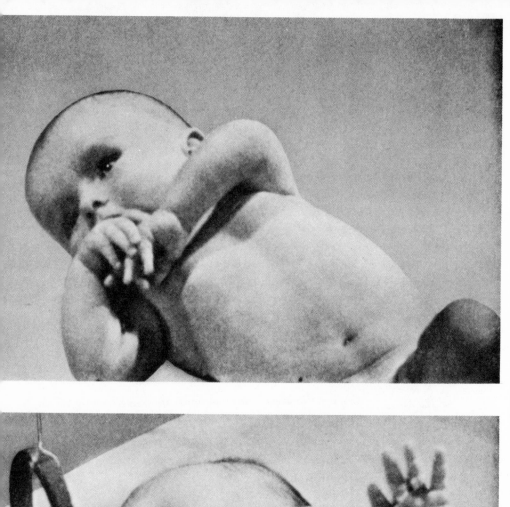

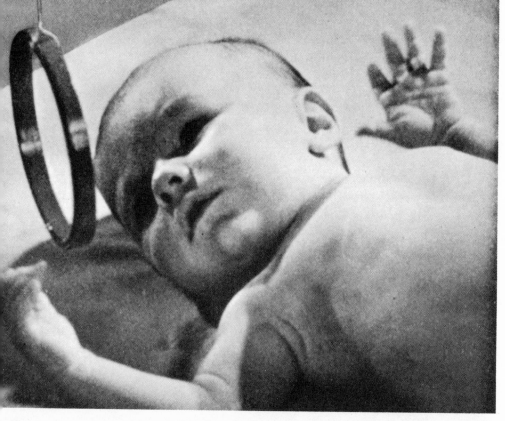

A one-inch cube reveals his eye-hand co-ordination at the age of four months.
He moves his eyes, selectively: he looks from cube to hand and then back again from hand to cube.

His eyes fasten upon the test object, and they maintain a firm grasp. The hands are activated even though they cannot as yet obey precisely.

It is again evident that the eyes have a top priority in the scheme of development.
He can reach with his eyes—but not with his hands.

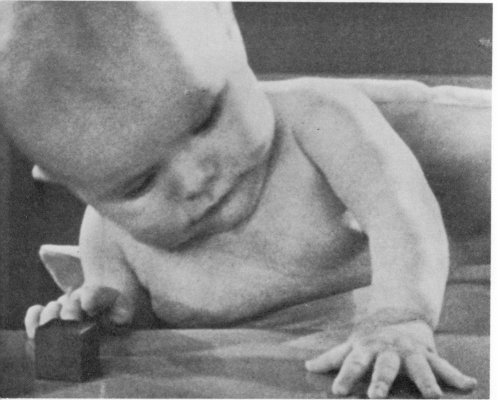

Growth Cycle   Ages: 7 months and 9 months

Two months later, at twenty-four weeks of age, he can reach with his hands; he contacts the cube with a precarious palmar grasp, he fumbles, but vision and touch are coming into correlation.

At seven months of age, prehension is much less crude: the fingers close upon the cube with decision.
A new and most significant pattern of behavior emerges spontaneously: transfer from hand to hand.
The infant transfers the cube from one hand to the other, and retransfers.

The nine-month-old infant reaches on sight—with dispatch.
His grasp is more delicate, more digital.
Vertical banging is being replaced by horizontal rubbing.
Exploitively he brings two cubes into productive combination.

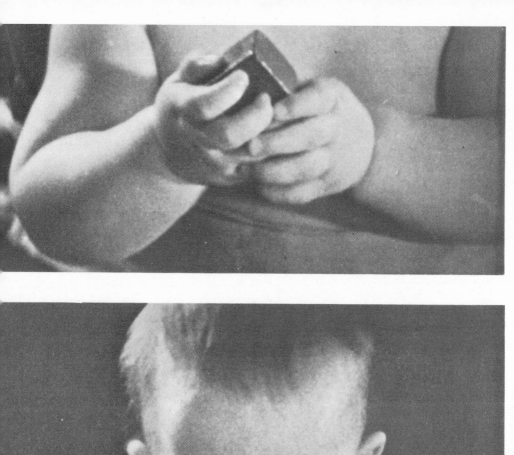

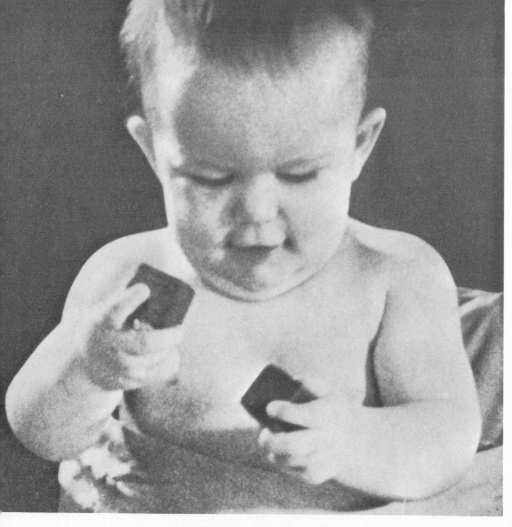

Visual grasp, manual grasp, and manipulation mature in close inter-action.
There is increasing refinement of eye-hand co-ordination.

The hand of the young infant remains fisted for weeks, lacking cortical control.
The eyes, however, are alert and take hold early, while manual grasp is still primitive and pawlike.

Here in stop motion the middle fingers crudely grip the cube.

At a later stage the forefinger and the thumb come into play, with ever-increasing dexterity.

By the end of the first year the infant grasps with finger tips, oppos-ing thumb to forefinger, and forefinger to thumb.

Growth Cycle Ages: 1½, 2, and 3 years

By eighteen months he exhibits almost adult skill.
He can release a cube at will with purpose and intent—maturing cortical control.
He places one block upon another: evidence of his growing mastery of spatial relationships.

At eighteen months he commands the vertical dimension: he builds a tower.

By two years of age he favors the horizontal dimension: he builds a wall.

By three years, a bridge, combining the vertical and horizontal.
Command of the oblique must wait.

Growth Cycle   Ages: 4, 7, and 10 months

There is a geometry of growth in the conquest of space.
Compared with the cube, the tiny pellet requires refinement of eye
and hand co-ordination.

*It's a small pellet, but it stirs the whole being of this four-month-old
infant*
He picks up the pellet with his eyes and does not relax his attention.
He glances at his hands, but he cannot bring them under control.
It will take a half year of growth before he can pick up the test
pellet with fingers as neatly as he now does with his eyes.

*At about seven months he makes a direct approach, all fingers out-
spread.*
He rakes and he contacts, but he cannot grasp the pellet.

*At about ten months the maturing nervous system prompts him to
probe with index finger—a refinement which leads toward precise
prehension.*
Thumb and index come into increasing opposition. . . .
Soon he plucks the pellet with pincer grasp and completes the
pattern, hand to mouth.

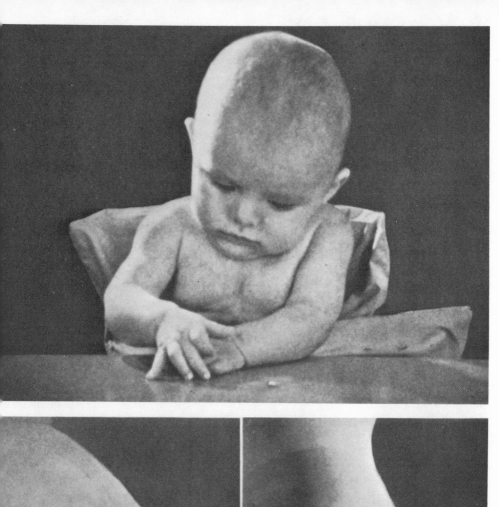
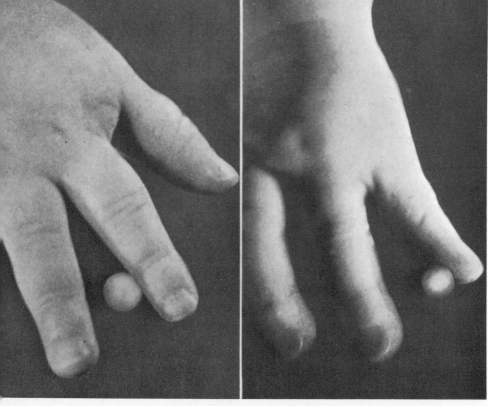

Growth Cycle   Ages: Prenatal and Postnatal

*Behavior patterns are neurologically organized by a
process called reciprocal interweaving*

Reciprocal interweaving, symbolized by this moving light [depicted
in animation], is the growth process which brings into working balance the vast and dual networks of central and autonomic nervous
systems.

*The human organism is built on a bilateral basis: two hemispheres
of the brain . . . two eyes . . . two arms . . . two legs. . . .
This duality demands that each side be structurally and functionally
interwoven with its paired opposite.*

Growth, therefore, does not advance in a straight line.
It shuttles back and forth:
    Now accenting the right . . . now the left hemisphere. . . .
    The tonic-neck reflex at one age . . . the symmetro-tonic reflex
      later.
    Extension dominant at one age . . . flexion dominant at another.
    Grasp . . . and then release.
    Monocular fixation at one age . . . binocular fixation at another.

The central nervous system interweaves its dualities progressively.
*The organizing process follows an ascending path of maturation to
create an integrated organism, a total action system symbolized by
this spiral.*

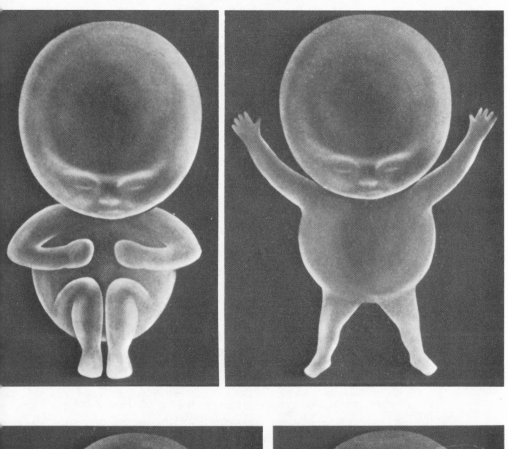

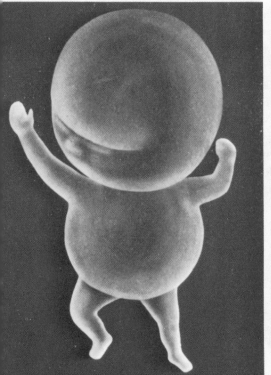

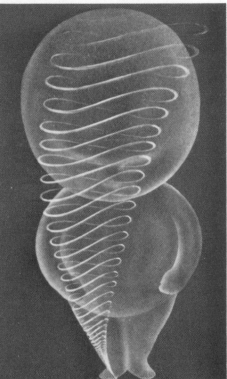

Growth Cycle   Ages: 10 months and 18 months

The principle of reciprocal interweaving pervades the entire embryology of behavior.

The newborn infant, prone and helpless, can be visualized against a background of many interwoven growth spirals.

Stage by stage, he brings flexors and extensors into reciprocal relationship: he crawls; he creeps on all fours.
In his own time he rises to the upright.
He toddles, walks, steps forth—a biped.

The newborn infant wages a contest with gravity. In a short year he retraces, in telescoped time, the evolutionary ascent of man.
This upward striving has one developmental goal: the release of eyes and hands for higher uses. . . .

At about ten months of age the creeping infant is under an irresistible urge to pull himself to his feet.

In due course he casts off his mooring and strides the earth, a potential maker and user of tools—his eyes and hands emancipated. His hands are now free to wield a crayon.

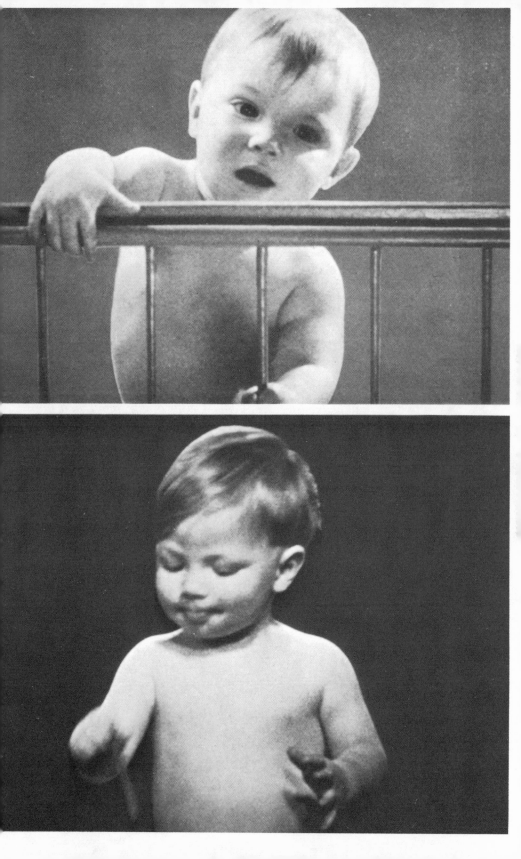

Growth Cycle   Ages: 2, 2½, 3, 4, 5 years

At eighteen months he scribbles.

At about two years he executes a vertical stroke.

At two and a half years, a horizontal stroke.

*At three and four years, a cross, combining vertical and horizontal—
and a circle.*

At five, a triangle, leading to advanced skills of eye, hand, and brain.

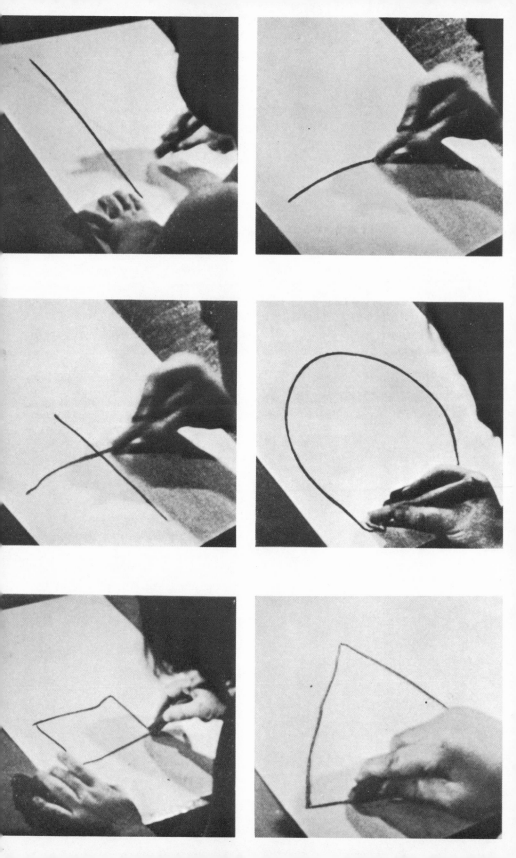

Growth Cycle Age: 7 months

The physician has a valuable clinical tool in the methods and procedure of developmental diagnosis

This infant has been referred for a developmental examination at the age of seven months.

Graded tests of behavior and standardized test materials are applied to determine the maturity and the integrity of his nervous system. His reactions to the test cube—grasp, mouthing, inspection, banging —are typical of the seven months' level of maturity.

These behavior patterns denote a normal development of eye-hand co-ordination.

Growth Cycle Ages: 18, 12, and 18 months

This boy, eighteen months old, shows an extreme degree of retardation in eye-hand behavior.

He looks at the cube, but he cannot grasp it.
He looks from cube to hand, from hand to cube—a behavior pattern which indicates a four months' level of maturity.

Here is a one-year-old boy who can grasp and transfer a cube, but whose whole total behavior is poorly organized. Attentional patterns are faulty. *Eyes and hands frequently fail to co-ordinate. He assumes stereotyped postures, which indicate a defectively integrated personality.* This child is eighteen months old. She presents a more nearly integrated action system. *She grasps, transfers, and manipulates at a seven months' level of performance.* She exploits a single cube with fairly sustained attention. However, like a seven-month-old infant, she shows no capacity to bring two cubes into productive combination.
Motor co-ordination is relatively normal; adaptive behavior is defective.

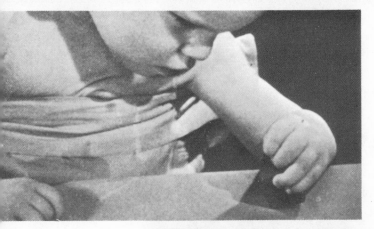

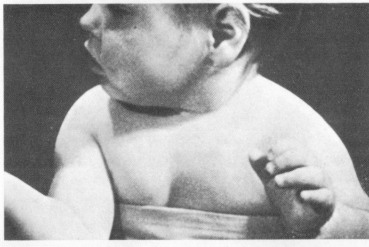

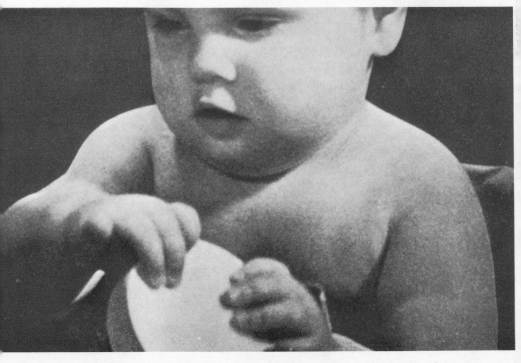

Growth Cycle Ages: 18 and 16 months

In this boy, of similar age, with cerebral palsy, the motor functions are damaged, but adaptive behavior is significantly normal in character.

In spite of athetosis and spasticity, he displays interest, drive, and purposefulness in his exploitation of the consecutive cubes, releasing them one by one.

The diagnostic cubes and form-board reveal neurological damage, but they also reveal normal growth potentials. . . .

Normal growth potentials comparable to those of this boy whose motor abilities are obviously undamaged.

The methods of developmental diagnosis can be used in behalf of all types of children: handicapped, gifted, maladjusted, retarded, and normal.

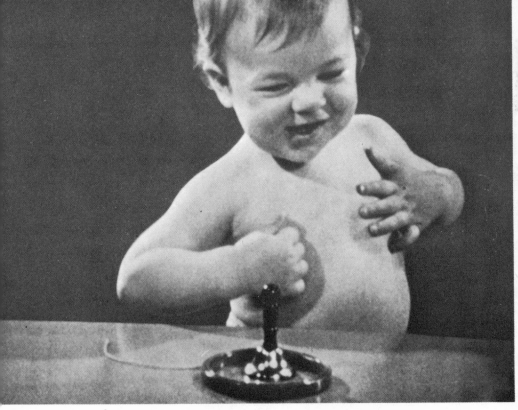

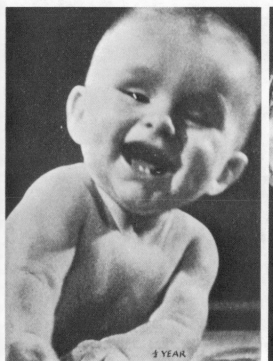

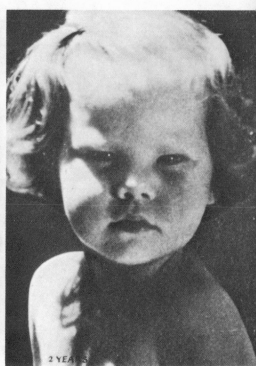

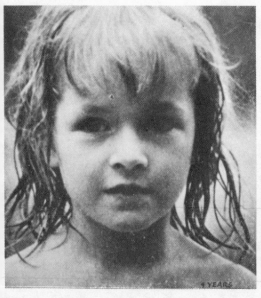

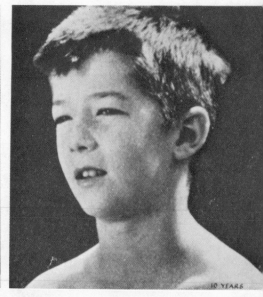

END TITLE

Behavior grows. Behavior assumes characteristic patterns. Every child has a unique
pattern of growth, which is the key to his
individuality. The race evolves; the child
grows; the human species and the individual alike are subject to an intrinsic embryology of behavior.

CHAPTER THREE

The Human Action System
in Evolution

The Origins of Growth Potentials and Patterns

The race evolves; the child grows. In this aphorism we have more than a hint of how the human infant has come into possession of his prodigious powers of development.

Human infancy is pre-eminently a period of genesis and growth. But the genesis of this genesis must be sought in the vastly longer period of organic evolution. The human infant is in a true sense the focal end product of countless ages of racial prehistory. Infancy was evolved to subserve the needs of growth for the individual and to supply the conditions of continuing evolution for the race.

Every infant, accordingly, comes into the world with potentialities of growth which perpetuate the essential traits of the species. He is also endowed with a margin of modifiability which makes for innovation and mutation. No one needs to teach him how to grow. The capacity to grow is an intrinsic part of the instinct to survive. The tendency of all growth, handicapped as well as normal, is toward an optimal realization, and Nature is prolonging the period of human infancy to permit a wider and, we hope, a higher range of realization. Accordingly, it takes the modern infant a long time to grow up, both biologically and culturally. It takes over twenty years of ontogenetic time, because it took aeons of phyletic (evolutionary) time to bring the human action system to its present level of complexity.

The term *action system* is very serviceable because it can be used flexibly either in a structural or a functional sense. It denotes the total organism as a going concern, particularly its behavior capacities, propensities, and patterns.

The human action system is fearfully and wonderfully made. It

43

includes the vegetative and regulative functions controlled by autonomic nerve nets in close correlation with the highest functions mediated by eyes, hands, larynx, and brain. This intricate, integrated action system was long in the making. A glance at its evolutionary history will show whence the human infant derives his profound powers of growth. It has taken unnumbered generations to fashion his behavior equipment and his behavior potentials. . . .

Over a billion years ago the earth cooled off sufficiently to support primitive forms of aquatic life. There were early worms with photochemical substance in their side walls. Pre-Cambrian mollusks acquired lenses, and Devonian fish were equipped with eyes which bear a rather startling resemblance to our very own. Not startling, however, to the anthropologist who blithely reminds us that man is but a modified fish!

The human eye did indeed originate in water, and was anciently foreshadowed in the fish. Consider a typical fish. It has no neck to speak of, and is therefore below the phyletic threshold of the tonic-neck-reflex. But the fish eye is, nevertheless, equipped with a full set of oculomotor muscles, internal, external, and oblique. The function of these muscles is to maintain a motionless panorama. This enables the fish to detect a movement denoting food or foe. Not having a neck, the fish turns its whole body in order to keep the object of interest within a narrow binocular field. The field is narrow because a fish wears its eyes on the side.

In the course of evolution the eyes moved forward to a frontal position. Terrestrial successors of the fish acquired a neck for head rotation and limbs for locomotion. Ground-going quadrupeds tread the earth on smooth-walking pads. In primates and preprimates who tended to assume more or less erect postures the forelimbs were increasingly used for grasping and manipulation. The volar pads were replaced by friction ridges (skin patterns), which served especially to enhance the efficacy of the hand as a sensorimotor organ of prehension and of exploitive touch. In the higher creatures snout and smell receded to give greater scope to vision. Eye, hand, and brain thereby came into new relationships in the evolution of what was to become the human action system.

The vast changes which we have summed up in a brief paragraph are reflected in the development of the human fetus. The aforementioned volar pads first appear at about the sixth week of development when the hand is rayed, but still paddlelike. They are prominent at the fetal age of ten weeks; then they begin to regress after the age of twelve weeks, when the friction ridges start to differentiate, becoming elevated above the skin near the eighteenth week. Once formed, the patterns of the ridges are fixed indelibly for life. Thus the fingerprint which uniquely identifies the individual is laid down before the middle of gestation. The first movements of the fetal eyes and hands, as we shall see, likewise occur prior to the eighteenth week. It is evident that the primary manifestations of growth, whether physical or functional, have their origin and to some degree even their form in the antecedents of racial evolution.

Fifty million years ago a preprimate, similar to *tarsius spectrum*, had come upon the scene—a furry arboreal creature, somewhat smaller than a kitten, with enormous eyes and a pair of delicate hands. Sitting upright *tarsius* used these hands in a squirrel-like manner to hold, to manipulate and nibble a food morsel. This hand-to-mouth-to-eye-to-hand-to-mouth behavior pattern involved an enormous expansion of the occipital, visual areas of the brain. Vision, thenceforth, was destined to become the leading sense in the evolution of the action system.

All that has happened since to the anthropoid-humanoid stocks which emerged after the Eocene tarsiers has tended to enhance and to enrich the visual functions. The brain nucleus, which governs visual accommodation, was remodeled in the primates and was split so that each eye can be focused independently upon any object. This opened the way to progressive refinements in visual perception. The eyes increased in adaptability without becoming overspecialized. The hands likewise underwent functional refinements, within a primitive ground plan, and without excessive specialization. The foot, however, became the most specialized and distinctive feature of human anatomy. The feet became arch platforms which enabled man to maintain an erect posture and to walk the earth, a conqueror, eyes forward.

Recent fossil finds in South Africa indicate that seven million years ago there lived a prehuman plesianthropos who walked somewhat erect. Presumably his forelimbs, even though they did not flex freely at the elbow, were sufficiently mobile to release hands and eyes for further evolutionary advance in the manipulations of matter and space. Each advance was embodied in the structure of the total action system. Vision became the guiding cue for the emancipated hands and they in turn directed the eyes through the co-ordinating facilities of the cerebral neurons.

In the fullness of time early man emerged, a maker and user of tools. Implements of stone have been found which may date back to the beginning of the pleistocene era, a full million years ago. These implements—pointed fist axes, choppers, knives, and hide scrapers—were fashioned from flint by strokes of a hammerstone. They were not accidents; they denoted a purposeful co-ordination of eye and hand.

The human hand harbored great potentialities. It was in itself a veritable kit of tools, a system of levers which could be flexed or extended more or less at will. At first doubtless the finger movements were crude and scarcely separated from shoulder and arm movements. The hand curled into a fist and the fingers moved conjointly. The fist could point, rub to and fro, and even swirl in circles through shoulder motion. In time the wrist became more flexible and the fingers moved independently. The thumb swept in with a sidewise pincer movement to pluck small objects. The index finger participated in this thumb opposition and acquired a significant priority, both sensory and motor, among the digits. It became specialized as the *fore*-finger to probe and to pry.

In some such manner the primitive hand became sophisticated. The progressive stages are mirrored in the eye-hand patterns which the human infant of today displays in the first year of life. The zeal with which he utilizes these patterns testifies to their deep origins in the prehistory of the race.

A large proportion of the infant's spontaneous activity—and for the infant, play is his self-chosen work—is devoted to the organization of his visual and manual behavior. He is not born with complete and automatic space perception. His visual-space world is built up by degrees. It is a product of slow and complicated growth aided but not initiated by experience. The visual domain of early man underwent a comparable evolution throughout hundreds of thousands of years. His visual insight and manual skills probably increased by slow gradations, as he exploited the manageable features of stones and the more plastic properties of clay, sand, water, wood, leaves, roots, bark, and trailing vines. He lifted, he placed and replaced, he poked (with his intrusive, inquisitive index finger); he pounded, pushed, pulled, arranged, and rearranged. He converted sticks and stones into tools. His manipulations of space became more elaborate as he produced permanent artifacts, as he stabilized his physical surroundings, and as he acquired (through evolution) an increasing number of planes of visual regard. Visual and motor reactions gave him the cybernetic feedbacks for practical judgments and for communication. His emotional life expressed in instinctive attitudes and feelings underwent comparable and associated evolutionary changes.

Some twenty-five thousand years ago less primitive man began to project visual and motor images upon external surfaces. He traced outlines and painted pictures on cave walls and on the hides of beasts. Some fifteen thousand years ago his graphic and plastic art reached a marvelous development. Cro-Magnon artists worked with sure strokes; they etched silhouettes of bison and mammoth on limestone, modeled figures in clay, and painted polychrome murals, using yellow, red, and black with vivid effects. Some seven thousand years ago pictures became symbols and signatures as well as portrayals. About five thousand years ago men began to record events and to write. Reading followed, but it was genetically rooted in recording. Civilizations now came into being.

The human action system—and notably the eye-hand-brain complex—had at long last reached a level of performance which enabled the race to build up a culture, embodied in material constructions and transmitted by language, tradition, and technologies. The modern infant born into this culture feels its intimate impacts from the moment of birth.

These impacts exert a far-reaching influence on the patterning of behavior, but at every turn that influence is delimited and configured by the inherent growth potentials which were built into the organism by the forces of evolution operating through vast stretches of time. The infant in brief, telescoped time becomes adapted to his cultural environment by a process which anthropologists might call *acculturation*.

We have sketched in broad outline the evolution of the human action system, to indicate the true source of the patterned energies manifested in the growth characteristics of the individual child. As a member of the species *Homo sapiens*, he develops in accordance with a general ground plan. As an individual descendant of parents and grandparents he develops in accordance with distinctive variations of the ground plan. He comes into his racial-familial inheritance through innate processes of growth which are called *maturation*. Maturation is mediated by genes.

The processes of acculturation and of maturation interact and interfuse, but the mechanisms of maturation are so fundamental that they are not transcended. In the following chapter we shall see how significantly the embryology of eye-hand behavior reflects the venerable prehistory of the human action system.

CHAPTER FOUR

Eyes, Hands, and Brain

Stages and Ages in Ontogenetic Sequence

The human infant in his ontogenetic cycle of growth sums up in his own manner the vast evolutionary antecedents which brought him into being. This is most clearly evidenced in the developmental morphology of his eye-hand behavior, as already indicated in a previous chapter. The present chapter will set forth in more detail the advancing stages of growth whereby the human *action system* through eyes and hands achieves progressive adaptations to the forces of light and gravity.

FETAL PERIOD

The story of these stages begins very early. Five weeks after conception, when the human embryo has a crown-rump length of approximately five millimeters, the three primary brain vesicles, the optic cups, and the limb buds have already taken form. Even the digits have begun to differentiate; and incidentally, it is interesting to note that the radial digits take the lead in this early differentiation. In later life, when the embryo has become an active year-old infant, these same radial digits will have attained an important pre-eminence over the other digits. The pre-eminence is prefigured in the somatic precocity manifested in the fifth week of gestation.

Functional precocities likewise occur remarkably early in the uterine period. Between the tenth and the fifteenth week of gestation a large number of responsive and spontaneous behavior patterns have been identified, notably by the observations of Davenport Hooker. Fingers fan, close, flex (on palm stimulation). Eyes move beneath fused lids; the lids also contract in a winklike manner. The head flexes, extends, rotates; the wrists flex and extend; the arms rotate and approximate by simultaneous adduction. Many of these fetal reactions simulate later patterns of infant behavior. They not only represent necessary preliminary stages; more often they constitute basic components of the eventual postnatal patterns. By the fetal age of twenty weeks, aversion of the head tends to induce a movement of the arm on the averted side. By twenty-eight weeks of fetal age a well-defined tonic-neck-reflex pattern can be observed in a viable prematurely born infant. This important pattern undergoes further developments in the elaboration of the eye-hand-brain complex for months and even years to come. Throughout the fetal period muscle tonus not only increases in amount but organizes into appropriate patterns, requisite for postnatal life. This is Nature's method of fore-reference. It is an arresting fact that for six months prior to birth, and before their first exposure to light, the eyes of the fetus recurrently move in their orbits by way of preparation.

Little is known about the nature of the prenatal eye movements. Although those movements are not occasioned by light stimulus, they may well be influenced by postural orientations. They undoubtedly become progressively co-ordinated toward the end of the gestation period. Accordingly, the eyes of the newborn infant move conjugately from side to side, soon after birth. He is also capable of co-ordinate compensatory eye movements, by means of which constant fixation of a stationary object is maintained during rotation of the head. A moving object is pursued with saccadic eye movements, which become increasingly proficient during the first two months. Even during sustained fixation of a fixed object, the eyes are never absolutely steady, but make minute horizontal and vertical excursions which cause the fovea to traverse different parts of the stimulus object. Such ocular excursions also figure in the infant's perception of form.

The seeing eye, therefore, is by no means a passive receptor organ. It is a highly active, kinetic organ, which exercises motor initiative, which seeks out and takes ocular hold of objects of interest. As a sensorimotor system, the visual apparatus is conjointly concerned with light, space, and gravity. The groundwork for the complex postnatal patterns of visual behavior is thus laid down during the uterine period.

Eye postures are significantly related to body postures. Through elaborate nerve connections the eyes are linked with the semicircular canals where endolymph reacts to the pulls of gravity and thereby influences the positions of the eyes, head carriage, and limb tonus.

Since the labyrinth is differentiated in the.human fetus as early as the tenth week, it is quite possible that some of the early movements of the eyes are occasioned by changes of bodily position of fetus in space. This primitive vestibular system operates at a lower neurological level than the visual system, which is mediated by the brain cortex with the superior colliculus functioning as an extremely elaborate sensory receptive area.

Human vision outranks all the other senses in the abundance of its sensory, motor, autonomic, and higher cortical ramifications. There are a million fibers in the optic nerve and they have vast representation within both the ancient brain and the neopallium. Each eye has more than 100,000,000 photoreceptors in the retina, which consists of highly specialized neurons. The retina has been likened to an island of the central nervous system with a cable of incoming and outgoing nerve fibers establishing connection with the main body. The retina is indeed both an outgrowth and an outpost of the brain. Up to about the eighteenth week of its fetal development there is a striking correspondence between the several layers of the retina and of the brain cortex.

The retinal layers begin to differentiate at about the sixth week. Interestingly enough, the upper half differentiates in advance of the lower, because the lower is phylogenetically younger. The macula (not present in the fish) begins its differentiation near the twelfth week, and at the twenty-fourth week the ganglion cells of the retina recede to form a central pit, the *fovea centralis*, beset with specialized cones. This important structure will undergo further developments in the first half year of infancy; but at the time of its formation, the twenty-fourth fetal week, the *fovea* is already as far distant from the optic nerve head as it will be in the adult eye. This is a remarkable fact when one considers the extensive anatomical changes which are yet to follow during the remaining half of the gestation period and throughout the postnatal period of growth. The eye itself will more than double its weight prior to birth. It and the brain will increase three and one-half times from birth to maturity, and the body will increase twenty-one times. Nevertheless, the distance between *fovea* and nerve head, established at twenty-four weeks, remains an absolute.

This certifies to the profound importance of vision in the embryology of human behavior. The macula becomes a fixed pivot in the whole process of morphogenesis.

The fetal eyes begin to open at about the twenty-fourth week after conception. By this time the infant-to-be is in possession of his full quota of neurons, some ten or twelve billions in number. The rods and cones have differentiated and the visual pathway from retina to cerebral centers is completed in another month. An infant born ten or twelve weeks prematurely therefore shows definite visual awareness; he blinks and frowns to a bright light. His fingers flex slightly on tactile pressure of a rod inserted in the palm. He may assume a tonic-neck-reflex attitude, but the general body tone is not firmly consolidated. It fluctuates unevenly. His postural movements are sporadic and meager. In a few weeks his tonic-neck-reflex becomes more defined. Occasionally he activates the extended arm with a windmill movement. His muscular tone is now more steady and responsive. His fingers clench and nails blanch on palmar stimulation. Generally the hands remain closed in tonic flexion. He is somewhat less torporous; he opens his eyes oftener and more widely. He does not fixate upon a near object, but his eyes respond to the dangling ring with a momentary, saccadic after-pursuit. With each week the waking interludes increase in length and move toward a diurnal pattern. The ability to wake up, like all complex behaviors, is based upon morphogenetic changes in the central nervous system. The waking propensity requires special neurological arrangements which, in the circumnatal period, are probably organized in the thalamic region of the brain—the equivalent, according to Kleitmann, of a primitive waking center.

Uncomplicated prematurity exacts no marked penalty. It demonstrates the lawfulness and stability of the maturational factors in the embryology of behavior. Prematurity displaces the time of birth, but it does not thereby permanently dislocate the basic sequences of development when the sequences are reckoned from the time of conception. Gestation age represents the length of time the fetus has been in the uterus. It can be estimated by various criteria, and a corrected chronological age can be calculated by discounting the weeks of prematurity. When appraised in terms of corrected age, the course of behavior patterning tends to parallel that of the full-term infant.

The behavior patterning observable in the fetal-infant from the twenty-eighth to the fortieth week of fetal age demonstrates the continuity and essential identities of uterine and post-uterine development. In tracing the subsequent course of eye-hand behavior developments it will be convenient to refer to five key age periods based on lunar-month intervals as follows: (1) Neonatal period (0-4 weeks); (2) First Quarter (4-16 weeks); (3) Second Quarter (16-28 weeks); (4) Third Quarter (28-40 weeks); (5) Fourth Quarter (40-52 weeks).

In perspective, the trends of development are somewhat as follows: In the first quarter the infant gains basic control of eye movements. He favors supine prone postures. In the second quarter he gains command of head station and attains an elementary co-ordination of eyes and hands; he grasps crudely. In the third quarter he acquires increased control of trunk and fingers; he sits; he manipulates objects. In the fourth quarter his command extends to legs and feet, and finger tips, with specialized adaptations of forefinger and thumb. He stands; he plucks and probes. All these progressive co-ordinations of eyes, hands, and postures are based on changes in brain structure which began long before birth.

THE NEONATAL PERIOD

The neonatal period (0-4 weeks) is of necessity a critical transition for all infants able to meet the challenge of birth. The challenge must be met at a biochemical level and at a behavioral level. Both levels are inextricably involved in achieving "homeostasis," the co-ordinated physiological mechanism whereby the organ systems co-operate to produce the steady internal environment on which life, growth, and behavior depend. The nervous system, both autonomic and cerebrospinal, participates in the regulation of the processes which include body temperature, nutrition and sleep, and the equilibration of body fluids. Difficulties in the regulation of body economy are reflected in unsteady, fluctuating, and exaggerated responses. Nevertheless, in the normal infant the over-all trend is toward stability.

The behavior development in the first four weeks is in no sense chaotic and formless. Visual behavior undergoes a remarkable degree of organization. Conjugate and co-ordinate compensation eye movements occur soon after birth. Brief fixations of an approaching near object occur in the first week; sustained fixation, by the end of the first month. In its early stages, as demonstrated by the studies of Ling, the fixation is typically monocular. The active eye immobilizes except for minute lateral and vertical movements. The other eye rests or wanders willy-nilly. At a later stage the monocular fixation alternates rapidly from eye to eye and this leads developmentally into binocular convergence at about the second month.

Vision plays a prominent role in the mental life of the neonate. He experiences eye movements, kinesthetically, as he makes them; recurrently he halts these movements with an intent ocular fixation. He regards a nearby face in a manner which suggests interest and a nascent kind of attention. His visual "ego" first organizes at near point, and outward from near point the visual domain long continues to develop. His hands, however, are predominantly closed, even when his eyes are open. Yet if one touches the fist the activity of the arm increases and the hand clenches or opens. The mouth, a more primitive organ of prehension, is temporarily more advanced than the hands.

LATER POSTNATAL PERIOD

During the first quarter (4-16 weeks), visual functions continue to play a leading role in the developmental psychology of the infant. With small but rapid conjugate eye movements—lateral, vertical, and oblique—he explores the contour of near objects of interest. With increasingly facile roving movements, his eyes inspect his surroundings. He has a veritable hunger for visual experiences. He may even fret if the hunger is not satisfied. Repeatedly and often prolongedly he gazes in the direction of his extended arm, as though regarding his own hand. The t-n-r (tonic-neck-reflex) attitude to which he is addicted channelizes visual fixation. In due course it leads to reaching on sight, with directed looking after the object is grasped.

At sixteen weeks he already enjoys the visual-motor tests of a behavior examination. Propped in a supportive chair in front of the test table, he gives ample evidence that the cube before him is an object of visual interest. He holds his head steady; he looks at table top, at cube, at his own hand; he scratches (foretoken of prehension); he renews his reactions in an almost circular manner. Eye-hand co-ordination is actively in the making.

On the basis of our normative data it is possible to draw up a condensed tabular summary of the growth gradient whereby the infant achieves and perfects his eye-hand co-ordinations. The growth of behavior patterns is typified in the reactions to a red one-inch cube as a standardized stimulus object. Approximate ages for the first year are given in weeks at lunar-month intervals. (The infant is seated at a test table.)

12 weeks—Regards cube momentarily.
16 weeks—Looks from hand to cube to hand.
20 weeks—Grasps cube on contact (tactile).
24 weeks—Reaches and grasps on sight.
28 weeks—Transfers cube from hand to hand.
32 weeks—Grasps a cube with one hand and then a second cube with the other.
36 weeks—Pushes one cube on table with another cube.
40 weeks—Combines two cubes, one in either hand.
44 weeks—Removes cube from cup, and inserts without release.
48 weeks—Picks up and releases several cubes one by one.
52 weeks—Releases cube in cup.
15 months—Builds a tower of 2 cubes.
18 months—Builds a tower of 3 cubes (vertical array).
24 months—Builds a wall of 3 cubes (horizontal).
36 months—Builds a bridge of 3 cubes (combining vertical and horizontal).

The infant at all these ages is under an irrepressible impulse to appropriate the cube (by eyes and hands) and to exploit it once it is seized. The cube then becomes an implement and an extension of his action system. The resultant behavior patterns reflect the manner in which the race cumulatively mastered the elementary physics and mathematics of its environment. In a condensed telescoped version the infant reminds us how ancient man gradually became a tool user.

In the race and in the child alike the contrivance and use of tools are closely correlated with the genesis of practical reasoning and of rudimentary concepts of geometry and engineering. The cube behavior patterns of the growing infant therefore reveal much more than mere motor skills. The ontogenetic sequence of these patterns tells us something about "the mind" in the making—the formation of judgments and generalizations based on an increasing perception of objects in relation to space, time and gravity.

The texture, shape, and surfaces of the cube are sensed through eyes, hands, and mouth working in co-operation. The transposability of objects in space is sensed and effected through transfer, pushing, dropping, resecuring, banging, poking, brandishing. These maneuvers are by no means chaotic; they are ordered by the directives of embryological growth, and they lead into increasingly discriminating manipulations and juxtapositions. The single cube gives way to a combinative interest in two cubes. The single cube is thrust into a hollow container (the cup), denoting a penetration into the third dimension of space.

Somewhat later the infant acquires the very important power of voluntary release of grasp. This opens a vast field of permutations in his eye-hand activity. He picks up one cube and releases it. He picks up *another* cube and releases it (*that makes two*). He picks up still another and releases it (*that makes three*). He is much too young to count by spoken words. But this one-by-one behavior is unquestionably the embryological root and prerequisite of later mathematical numeration and comprehension.

The rudiments of geometry are contained in his spontaneous progress from random to serial to vertical to horizontal and oblique arrangements of his building blocks. At eighteen months he aligns three blocks vertically. He must double his age before he can realign the same three blocks horizontally and vertically to build a bridge. Growth takes time.

The growth gradients which we have just sketched are typical of imumerable kinds of neuromotor behavior. The ground plan of eye-hand co-ordination is determined by the innate architecture of the growing nervous system. Marked deviations from this plan have significance for clinical neurology. But the normal infant proceeds with inborn propensity and assurance from stage to stage.

CHAPTER FIVE

The Total Action System

The Maturation of the Mind

From the standpoint of embryology we cannot readily separate mind from body nor body from mind. From the moment of conception the infant develops as a unit. He is a living organism "made of matter in space and actuated by energy in time." The organism functions at three levels: physiochemical, physiological, and behavioral; but the levels are so interdependent that it is difficult to define the emergence of the so-called "mind" and to state its relations to such near synonyms as personality, ego, self, psyche. The mind is not a separate indwelling entity nor a superadded agency. It is part and parcel of a unitary action system. It grows.

We are here chiefly concerned with the growth aspects. We need not speculate as to when and how consciousness begins; but we may grant, on the basis of objective signs, that even the young infant has a considerable degree of mental life. By the age of one month his behavior is too coherent, too integrated, and too personal in its individuality to be regarded as merely "subcortical." He manifests pleasure, pain, desire. He evidently senses comfort, discomfort, satiety, warmth. He responds to the touch of ministering hands; he heeds the human voice and face. He makes small throaty sounds which may already have a little improvisation. Some of his visual responses suggest acts of attention. Soon they will indicate actual volition. He is not an automaton whose activity consists of low-order reflexes, but an adaptive, changing, growing being—assimilative, explorative, and conscious on his plane of immaturity. He may well be capable of awarenesses which arise from processes of synthesis and integration. His "mind" is not larval. It is already in the making.

The infant's mental life must be inferred from the manner in which he grows up in a duplex world—a world of things and a world of persons. These two worlds are very closely associated in the period of infancy. It is therefore impossible to draw hard and fast lines between the four major fields of behavior: motor, adaptive, language, and personal-social. A glance at the early developments in these fields will serve to demonstrate the essential unity of the total action system.

MOTOR AND ADAPTIVE BEHAVIOR

We have already noted that thinking has part of its genesis in the sensorimotor activities of eyes and hands. These activities are spontaneous, and they display considerable resourcefulness. The exploitiveness of the infant's eager play testifies to deep-seated maturational factors. His restless inquisitiveness and manipulations are untaught. They primarily determine what and when he will learn through experience. Without training he places a cube into a cup at about the age of one year. He does it so spontaneously that the behavior looks "instinctive." It surely is adaptive behavior and perhaps we should call it intelligence, for intelligence is the capacity to initiate new experience, and to profit by the experience thus initiated.

Motor and adaptive behavior are intimately combined in early life, because under the pressure of growth, a normal infant feels impelled to put each newly attained motor ability to repetitive use, and to exercise it with experimental variations. For example, an eight-weeks-old infant can not reach for a rattle, but will briefly retain a rattle placed in his hand—a slight bit of adaptive behavior, which is not an altogether pure reflex. At twelve weeks he will hold the rattle actively and even glance in its direction. At sixteen weeks he regards it immediately and intently. He also deploys his eyes in a roving manner to "contact" his surroundings. In the next two months he reaches out to contact, to grasp and to hold. Thus by subtle growth stages which begin very early the infant's visual and manual behavior takes on voluntary and adaptive characteristics.

It is probable that all mental life has a motor basis and a motor origin. The non-mystical mind must always *take hold.* Even in the rarefied realms of conceptual reasoning we speak of intellectual *grasp* and of symbolic *apprehension.* Thinking might be defined as a *comprehension* and *manipulation* of meanings. Accordingly, thought has its beginnings in infancy. We have already noted the germ of mathematics which lies in the one-by-one behavior pattern of the year-old infant. Counting is based on serial motor manipulation.

LANGUAGE

Language likewise has a motor basis. Primitive language is mediated by postures, by facial expression, by manual gestures, and by vocalizations. Under the impress of culture the vocalizations become articulate, and the child learns to speak. Ultimately his words become vehicles of thoughts and even of trains of thought. His linguistic and intellectual *acculturation*, however, is limited at every turn by maturational factors.

The manner and the order in which a child acquires speech reflect stages and patterns of neuromuscular maturity. At four weeks of age his utterance, apart from crying, is restricted to small throaty sounds. At eight weeks he vocalizes single vowel sounds (ah, eh, uh). At twelve weeks he chuckles; at sixteen weeks, laughs; at twenty weeks, squeals. By twenty-eight weeks he usually is capable of making polysyllabic vowel sounds and a consonantal m-m-m. By the first year he imitates sounds, and has a word or two in his vocabulary. At fifteen months he frequently uses a jargon which seems formless but is configured by inflections and rhythms. The jargon is a developmental matrix for words which ordinarily begin to multiply in the period from eighteen months to two years. At two years, or soon thereafter, jargon is usually being displaced by three-word sentences, including the use of pronouns. At three years the child begins to use prepositions and plurals with some facility.

The ontogenesis of articulate utterance is complex. The correct production of each of the consonant and vowel sounds does not proceed from age to age in gradual advance toward specificity, but shifts with repeated regressions and progressions. The mastery of consonants in terms of phonetic placement progresses from labial to glottal to postdental to labial-dental, that is, from front to back to middle. Vowel sounds progress from back to front to middle. Maturational rather than environmental factors account for such trends.

Words, whether spoken or unspoken, are cultural devices for facilitating the expression and the manipulation of meanings. When an infant or child manipulates objects in a meaningful manner, even without overt or inner speech, he may nevertheless be thinking in his own self-absorbed way. But when he wishes to formulate a personal meaning to himself, or to communicate it socially to others, he uses in due course interjections, words, phrases, and sentences. His preverbal and verbal language alike is decisively influenced by the conventions of the culture in which he is bred, but it is nonetheless subject to the laws of development.

PERSONAL-SOCIAL BEHAVIOR

From the moment of birth the human infant feels the impacts of personal care. He grows up in a world of things and in a much more bewildering world of persons. For him the two worlds at first are virtually blended. Part of the task of development is to achieve a distinction between them. He must find himself in what would be a chaotic welter of stimuli were he not protected by the ordering forces of his own organic growth.

The newborn baby is all universality or all ego, as you may choose. His subjective self must be vaguely confined to the flow of sensory impressions which arise from the total area of his outer skin and the vaster mucous membranes of his inner skin. Here is the nucleus or core of a personal self which grows and elaborates with almost dramatic rapidity during the early years of life. This self is an organized and organizing web of behavior patterns—particularly of personal-social behavior. These patterns sum up his reactions to other persons in the culture which rears him.

His sensitivity to cultural impress is so great that his perception of other persons may at times seem to be in advance of the awareness of his private self. He is aware of the incoming and outgoing hand of his mother before he becomes acquainted with the movements of his own hand. He probably hears his mother's voice before he identifies his own spontaneous vocalizations as his very own. If he did not establish countless contacts with other human beings, he could scarcely acquire a personality recognizable either to himself or to others. The make-up of his personality depends upon the reciprocal, interpersonal relationships which he experiences from day to day and from age to age. But he himself contributes the essential initiatives and responses. His biological equipment sets the primary limits, directions, and modalities in which he reacts to his personal environments.

In sketchy outline it is possible to indicate the maturational stages whereby the growing self takes shape through interaction with other selves. The age levels which will be designated are not to be taken too rigidly. They are, however, based on observations of numerous children, and suggest typical trends.

As early as the age of four weeks the infant reacts to social overtures by a reduction of general activity; at eight weeks his face animates to the point of smiling; at twelve weeks he both vocalizes and smiles in social response. At sixteen weeks he is capable of spontaneously initiating a social smile, and he displays recognition signs on the sight of his mother. At twenty-four weeks he begins to discriminate strangers, and at thirty-two weeks he may withdraw from them. He soon exhibits a remarkable perceptiveness in reading facial expressions. Toward the end of the first year he participates increasingly in two-way nursery games.

At two years of age the child calls himself by his own name, and shows a new sense of possessiveness. At two and a half years he uses the pronoun "I" with imperiousness. He does not have himself well in hand, and has difficulty in distinguishing between mine and thine. He is discovering a new realm of opposites. Life is no longer a one-way street as it was at eighteen months, but is charged with double alternatives, and he finds it hard to make simple choices and decisions. This is essentially due to his immaturity, for at the age of three years he will take pleasure in making voluntary choices which lie within the range of his ability. Meanwhile, because of his bipolar confusions, the two-and-a-half-year-old tends to be variously impetuous, hesitant, "contrary," dawdling, defiant, or ritualistic. He needs skillful guidance, which is more readily given if one is aware of the developmental mechanisms responsible for this transitional stage of lessened or loosened equilibrium.

EMOTION AND AUTONOMIC REGULATION

From the standpoint of a monistic embryology, the emotional life of an individual is closely bound up with the patterning of personal-social behavior and associated autonomic regulations. Emotions have a highly subjective aspect, and they are often characterized as being the driving forces which determine personality. This easily leads to misconceptions concerning the nature of emotions. Emotions are not self-subsistent entities, which operate independently.

They are patterned phenomena inseparably bound up with the organization of the total action system.

Emotion is essentially the feeling of a motor attitude (and its systemic, biochemical correlates). This feeling has been identified with an intermediate stage of response arising out of a delay which occurs after the assumption of a preliminary motor or motor-mental attitude.

The patterning of the child's emotional life, therefore, changes with his perceptual insights and his personal-social adjustments, all of which have specific attitudinal manifestations. The individual patterns of these motor attitudes are thus fundamentally shaped by maturity factors. In this sense, there is no general emotion of fear, anxiety, jealousy, love, insecurity, or aggression. An "emotion" expresses a basic stage of maturity and a specific body state and an end product of previous life career. The influence of environment and of social experience is far-reaching, but it is delimited and partly defined by maturational determinants traceable to species, racial stock, and familial inheritance.

Emotions grow. We may illustrate by the growth changes of an infant at twenty-eight weeks. The twenty-eight-week-old infant discriminates visiting strangers, but usually he adapts to them easily. Amiably he permits himself to be shifted from one lap to another. He seems to take in a total situation, and alternates with fair ease between self-directed and socially referred activity. At thirty-two weeks he is not so self-contained. His reactions are less forthright and his face often wears a questioning, half-bewildered expression. He shows a new tentativeness and timidity in unaccustomed situations and needs more time to adjust to them. This is reflected in changed patterns of visual behavior. He watches with new penetration the actions and movements of people around him. He is more aware of sights (and sounds) in the next room—a dawning appreciation of distance and location. His attitudes are more sensitive and withdrawn. Such sensitiveness combined with assimilativeness is part of the over-all process of growth, which involves the visual functions of the total developing action system. Comparable changes in emotional maturity occur throughout the life cycle. Emotional patterns, no less than patterns of cube behavior, are subject to mechanisms of maturation.

These mechanisms operate not only in relation to the cerebrospinal division of the nervous system but to the autonomic networks, which mediate the physiology of mood, emotion, and temperament. Somewhat paradoxically, autonomic regulation is conjointly concerned with the maintenance of a homeostatic steady state and the bodily expression of variable emotional states. But these regulations involve the total action system. Cobb distinguishes three main subsystems which are activated in emotional behavior: the endocrines, the ancient visceral brain, and the more recent thalamo-neocortex. "Emotion may be thought of as a reaction resulting from the interaction of all three." The hypothalamus is described as the center for integrative motor impulses and as the head ganglion of the autonomic nervous system whose regulatory controls include metabolism, temperature, secretions and excretions, cardiovascular, genitourinary, and gastrointestinal functions, and also sleep and awakeness. Emotional life arises out of these regulatory activities in close association with the perceiving, remembering, and symbolizing of the neocortex.

The phyletic history of the brain and the physiological character of its present-day operations demonstrate that emotions cannot have a self-subsisting status. All emotions are formed and formative phenomena dependent upon the maturity of a growing total action system. The animistic connotations which cling so tenaciously to the idea of emotion will not give way unless we acknowledge the morphogenetic essence of the growth process.

CHAPTER SIX

The Growth Process

Mechanisms and Principles of Behavior Development

Growth is a process of organization. It is a unitary and an integrative process. If it were not unitary, the organism would lack wholeness; if it were not integrative, the organism would lack individuality.

Growth is a patterning process in which the mutual fitness of organism and environment is brought into progressive realization. Growth produces in dynamic sequence an ever-changing complex of particulate patterns; nevertheless it also perpetuates the integrity of a single total pattern. The ground plan of this pervasive total pattern is laid down by the genes with their remarkable capacity to propagate themselves and to reorganize the surrounding molecules. The sum total of the gene effects is manifested in the hidden mechanism of maturation.

THE MECHANISM OF MATURATION

The precise nature of the gene effects is, of course, not known, but their operation can be visualized in physical and in chemical terms. The growing organism can be regarded as a physicochemical system. The investigations of chemical embryology are exploring the metabolic basis of morphogenesis—the physiological role of nucleic acids and of induction phenomena in the production of physical forms. The growing organism can also be regarded as a bioelectric system. It is alive with polar and electropotential differences. An electrodynamic field manifests and maintains the total togetherness of the organism at all stages of its development. Thus the embryo is perfectly integrated even before it acquires an autonomic or a somatic nervous system. The central nervous system, however, is destined to become the dominant instrument in preserving the unity of the total organism in its cycle of development.

We are here concerned with the behavioral aspects of this cycle of development. We think of the organism as an action system, and of growth as a process of progressive organization which builds up a *corpus of behavior*. This corpus, although in itself invisible, has a reality which is evidenced in patterns of behavior. It has a dynamic morphology which is governed by principles of development.

Several closely related principles can be identified. They apply generally to the ontogenetic development of species traits, but they also apply specifically to many traits of individuality which diversify human behavior, in infant, child, and adult.

THE PRINCIPLE OF MOTOR PRIORITY AND FORE-REFERENCE

Much of the embryology of behavior can be interpreted in terms of posture. The human action system is a postural mechanism. All vertebrates have a neuromuscular system which operates upon a skeletal system and thereby determines orientations to the physical world—to light, sound, gravity, etc. By posture is meant the posture assumed by the body as a whole or by its members in order to execute a movement or to maintain an attitude. No sharp line can be drawn between attitude and action. Each presupposes the other. Both eventually entail tonal discharge of musculature, autonomic and somatic.

In embryogenesis, muscle function precedes neural; motor nerves are functional before sensory; and proprioception sensitivity antedates exteroception. Accordingly, the motor attitudes and initiatives of the organism are intrinsically determined. They are laid down in advance of actual experience and utilization. By way of preparation and fore-reference the basic neuromotor equipment for acts of prehension, locomotion, and perception is developed well before it is put to actual test.

This principle is so fundamental that virtually all behavior ontogenetically has a motor origin and aspect. Vision, for example, has a motor as well as sensory basis; likewise speech, mental imagery, and conceptual thought. Even emotions trace to motor attitudes and tensions.

THE PRINCIPLE OF DEVELOPMENTAL DIRECTION

The *action system* is a complex postural mechanism which undergoes increasing differentiations with increasing maturity. This differentiation is not haphazard nor fortuitous. It follows directional lines, which are in part determined by the directions of the underlying neuronic growth. The neuronic growth is obedient to polarities and metabolic gradients.

The longitudinal gradient of the mesoderm governs the general course of somatic and behavioral organization. The over-all trend is from head to foot (cephalo-caudad), and from axial to appendicular musculature (proximal-distal). In the hand the trend of innervation is from little finger to index and thumb (the ulnar-radial shift). These three major trends do not occur in a single comprehensive sweep, once and for all. They repeat at successive epochs with variations which impart a spiral character to the progressions of development.

The head is so precocious that at the close of the second fetal month the height of the head approximates the length of the trunk. At twenty weeks of (postnatal) age the head maintains a steady station, but the trunk is relatively flaccid. In due course the trunk stiffens, first at the cervical level, last at the lumbar. Eyes and mouth take a lead over hands and feet. Some twenty stages of prone behavior precede the assumption of upright posture. There are three sub-cycles in this head to foot advance: the first culminates in prone pivoting, the second in creeping, the third in walking.

Prehension and manipulation exhibit similar directionality phenomena. Grasp advances from gross palmar to ulnar, medial, and radial digital patterns. Thumb opposition itself exhibits comparable refinements of approach and execution. Predilections for horizontal, vertical, oblique, and clockwise or counterclockwise circumductions are governed by directional trends inherent in the architecture of the developing action system.

THE PRINCIPLE OF RECIPROCAL INTERWEAVING

This principle is so pervasive and so clarifying that it has already received notice in a previous chapter. The principle arises out of the dual construction of the action system and its consequent dual alternatives of function. A mere enumeration of some of these dualities of structure and of function will indicate the developmental necessity of bringing them all into some kind of counterbalance and co-ordination. Man is built on a duplex plan. Many of his organs are paired: eyes, ears, jaws, arms, legs, hands, feet. A similar duplexity is

present in the anatomy of the viscera, brain, heart, lungs, musculature, and nervous systems. This duplexity is reflected in life processes at every level of functioning—in the reciprocal antagonism of
flexor and extensor muscles, in excitation and inhibition of biochemical and behavioral responses, in acceleration and retardation
of physiologic reactions, in assertion and withdrawal behavior.

The "task" of development is to bring opposites into effective
counterpoise. Flexors and extensors are opposed, but through
growth they are brought into reciprocity. Sherrington formulated a
law of reciprocal innervation which states that the inhibition of one
set of muscles while the opposing muscles are in excitation is a condition for effective movement. The structural basis for this physiological mechanism is gradually built up by ontogenetic maturation. The
maturation is somewhat rhythmic: for a given period it stresses the
flexor component of a behavior pattern, and later the extensor, and
then again the flexor. It is essentially a kind of neurological interweaving which interlaces the opposing motor components. Accordingly, in the patterning of prone behavior about half of the stages
show a flexor dominance and the other half an extensor. The child
does not learn by sharply separated installments to pivot, to creep,
and to walk. He exhibits new patterns when the concealed neuromotor interweavings have geared him for the appropriate action.

The principle of reciprocal interweaving, however, is so ubiqui-
tous that it is by no means confined to gross postural and locomotor
behavior. It operates in the realm of emotions in so far as they are
dependent on motor attitudes. It operates in the sensorimotor
aspects of vision, where a host of double alternatives call for har-
monization and modulation: monocular vs. binocular fixation; near
vs. far focus; central vs. peripheral awareness; incoming vs. outgoing fusion; abductive vs. adductive eye movements; skeletal vs.
visceral components; left vs. right ocular dominance.

Ontogenetic organization does not advance on an even front. The
action system does not enlarge homogeneously like an expanding
balloon. Growth is more nearly comparable to an intricate braiding
process, in which multitudinous strands are interwoven into patterns
which are manifested in co-ordinating patterns of behavior. Although the details of this process are inconceivably complex, the
general principle of reciprocal interweaving is readily understand-
able because it conforms to the recognizable trends of development.
For a frame of reference the principle may be formulated as a law:

The organization of reciprocal relationships between two growing, counterpoised functions (such as flexion vs. extension) is evidenced, ontogenetically, by successive shifts in the ascendancy of one function over the other, with progressive integration and modulation of the resultant behavior patterns.

THE PRINCIPLE OF FUNCTIONAL ASYMMETRY

In spite of his bilateral construction, man does not face the world squarely on a frontal plane of symmetry. He confronts it at an angle and he makes his escapes, also obliquely. Nature evidently did not intend that he should be completely or uniformly ambidextrous. He has a preferred hand, a dominant eye, and a lead foot. Effective attentional adjustments require an asymmetric motor set for adequate focalization.

The mechanism of reciprocal interweaving does not produce perfect symmetry and balance between right and left members of the action system. It brings them into reciprocal relationships, but basic unilateral preferences and orientations are built into the action system in obedience to the necessity of functional asymmetry. The tonic-neck-reflex is a striking example of how this principle operates to preserve both bilateral and monolateral aptitudes. Perfect ambidexterity, if it exists, would be almost an abnormal anomaly.

Handedness is not a simple trait which is established at one time, once and for all. It is a focal symptom of the current state of a changing organism. It is subject to fluctuations in intensity during the early years. The subordinate hand assumes changing roles and temporarily may seem dominant, but over the long reach the handedness manifested in infancy proves predictive.

THE PRINCIPLE OF SELF-REGULATION

How does the organism react to the conditioning stimuli which impinge upon it from the moment of birth? How does it learn? How does it avoid excessive and deleterious learning? The principle of self-regulation which is based on Nature's protection of the total organism affords a partial answer to these questions.

The human infant is a storer and distributor of energy. This daily cycle of activity and rest reflects the way in which he husbands and extends his energies; it also reflects a method of growth, of self-regulation. He will learn only when he is developmentally ready. He will learn only what is appropriate to his state of readiness. His conditionability is delimited by the maturity and primacy of the total action pattern.

The growing action system is in a state of formative instability combined with a progressive movement toward stability. Growth gains represent consolidations of stability. Stability and variability coexist, not as contradictory opposites, but as mutual complements. The maturing organism oscillates between self-limiting poles as it advances. The forward thrusts are comparable to gropings which seek a pathway. The flowing stream of development thus finds its channels.

This is a somewhat figurative statement, but it gives a hint of how the infant manages to adjust to routines, to outgrow them, and to oppose them. His economy is basically governed by regulatory mechanisms which are untaught and inherent in his organism. Given a reasonable degree of freedom, he works out a schedule of sleep, naps, feedings, and play which changes with his level of maturity. During the first week after birth he sleeps most of the day and night. Gradually he develops a "wakefulness of choice." The total duration of sleep per day constantly fluctuates but steadily diminishes. The average amount of diurnal sleep may fall from nineteen hours at four weeks to thirteen hours in the fortieth week. The fluctuations are somewhat rhythmic in character.

Comparable self-regulatory fluctuations occur in other fields of behavior, particularly during periods of rapid growth. There is a tendency for stages of relative equilibrium to be followed by stages of lessened equilibrium when the organism makes new thrusts into the unknown. But normally these thrusts do not go too far because the integrity of the organism must be preserved. This is the principle of self-regulation.

THE PRINCIPLE OF OPTIMAL REALIZATION

Being the end product of ages of evolution, the human *action system* is endowed with deeply entrenched growth potentials. Under normal or near normal conditions growth is irrepressible. If for any reason, somatic or cultural, the growth potentials are impeded, obstructed, or damaged, insurance mechanisms come into play. Every breach in the normal complex of growth is filled through regeneration, substitutive or compensatory growth of some kind. Behavior growth in this sense tends toward a maximum realization.

Although neurons cannot by subdivision increase in number, the integrative function of the nervous system preserves the unity of the impaired organism. Insurance reserves are drawn upon whenever the organism is threatened, even when normal behavior cannot be consummated. Herein lies the urgency and the irresistibility of growth. Herein lies a life tendency which works toward a measure of adjustment, harmony, and completion even in the handicapped child.

These six principles serve to remind us that growth is indeed a process—a living process governed by lawful mechanisms. Although principles must of necessity be stated in general terms, they have an explanatory usefulness in analyzing the import of concrete behavior characteristics. To parent and teacher the developmental principles may suggest why a given child at a given age acts as he does. To the physician they have orientational value and are a distinct aid in the diagnosis of normality, of defects and deviations.

CHAPTER SEVEN

Individual Differences and Deviations

The Individuality of Growth Careers

The developmental principles which have been outlined in the foregoing chapter are so fundamental that they apply to the entire human species. Although they are universal in scope, they vary in the form and intensity of their operation, and thus they account for many developmental differences among individuals of the species. There is a basic ground plan of growth peculiar to the species, and always a variation of that ground plan distinctive for the individual. A recognition of these variations is of importance for understanding the nature and needs of individual children.

Inasmuch as the operation of the principles depends upon maturational mechanisms, the hereditary endowment of the individual plays a primary role in shaping his over-all pattern and style of growth. Environmental stresses, disease, injury and damage affect the organization of the growth complex, and the developmental principles afford a convenient scheme of reference for interpreting the influence of such contributing factors.

Genes, however, are responsible for the basic developmental trends of species traits and of an endless variety of familial traits and of individual deviations. The morphogenetic mechanisms which underly the principles of developmental directionality, reciprocal interweavings, and functional asymmetry are subject to intrinsic variations which produce differences in neuromotor make-up and demeanor. These differences are reflected in distinctive modes of motor reactivity, of postural and locomotor organization, and also in inborn attitudes and weaknesses. Innate imperfections in functional asymmetries may have a far-reaching effect upon the patterning of the action system. The principle of optimal realization is likewise affected by genetic factors. The inborn insurance reserves which protect the growth of the organism vary in number, strength,

71

and availability. They are most vigorous and abundant in the well endowed. By combining the six developmental principles it is possible to envisage the genetic basis of individuality in terms of the growth process.

The problem of individual differences and deviations may also be considered in terms of varieties of physique and temperament. There are three major body types: the roundish (soft body, short neck, small hands and feet), the squarish (firm body with rugged muscles), the spindly (delicate in construction). Individual differences in physique are manifested in mixtures of these and related bodily characteristics. Sheldon has distinguished three temperamental types: viscerotonic, somatotonic, and cerebrotonic. The temperamental traits combine in varying degrees in different individuals. The extreme viscerotonic has a good digestive tract. He is good-natured, relaxed, sociable, communicative. The pronounced somatotonic is active, energetic, assertive, noisy, and aggressive. The fragile cerebrotonic is restrained, inhibited, tense; he may prefer solitude to noise and company. He is sensitive and likely to have allergies. Aphoristically, and not altogether whimsically, Sheldon sums up as follows: "The *cerebrotonic* eats and exercises to attend. The *viscerotonic* attends and exercises to eat. The *somatotonic* eats and attends in order to exercise."

The mention of digestive tract, energy, and allergies reminds us that the deepest determinants of individuality are biochemical, metabolic, and physiological. Every individual has a more or less unique metabolic pattern, based in part on his endocrine make-up. The fact that some of these metabolic and biochemical conditions (like color blindness) are heritable is significant. When not specifically transmissible, many metabolic and physiological characteristics may nevertheless be constitutional. Innumerable differences and deviations in sensorimotor equipment are inevitably reflected in the patterns of behavior at high personal and interpersonal levels. With increasing refinement of physiological techniques, many of these basic differences will become ascertainable in infancy and early childhood. This will widen the scope and accuracy of developmental diagnosis as discussed in the chapter which follows. Many sensorimotor characteristics are open to clinical observation and appraisal.

Visual traits, for example, display a wide range of variation. Vision is man's supreme sense, and it is so complexly constituted that no two children see exactly alike. Moreover, it is so intricate that it takes years of ontogenetic organization to attain maturity— from the fetal period into adolescence. From the standpoint of a developmental optics, the patterning of visual behavior involves the entire organism. Physiologically and psychologically, the visual system is part and parcel of the total unifying *action system.*

Vision comprises three functional fields which almost from the beginning develop conjointly, though not uniformly. Arranged in a hierarchy these three major functions interact as follows:

(1) The *skeletal* component of the visual system *seeks and holds* an image.

(2) The *visceral* component *discriminates and defines* an image.

(3) The *cortical* component *unifies and interprets* an image.

These visual functions can be objectively studied by physiological methods and by the techniques of analytic optometry and ophthalmology. The interrelations of the functions show lawful trends through advancing stages of development. There are manifold normal, atypical, and defective manifestations.

Infants reveal their visual individualities in eye movements and postural attitudes. Variations in the tonic-neck-reflex posture and the symmetro-tonic reactions during the first six months are noteworthy. These postures, both quiescent and active, constitute a morphogenetic matrix for establishing co-ordinations and dominances in patterns of eye-hand behavior. Excessive hand regard, if not due to retarded development, may signify a myopic trend. Atypical and distorted patterns of prehension and manipulation may indicate cerebral injury.

Even in the absence of a refractive examination visual difficulties may come to expression in the preschool years, particularly when the child leaves the familiar confines of the home. If he has serious eye-hand ineptitudes he reveals them in his play activities, in postural demeanors, in his adjustments to a play group, in his use of cup and spoon, of crayon and paints, and in his response to picture books. He may show forms of caution and withdrawal which are primarily due to visual rather than emotional factors. Atypical personal-social relations with his companions may have a visual basis in faulty space manipulation.

There are important individual differences in the size of visual fields and in the relative sensitivity of peripheral and focal areas. Children with marked focal vision show a quicker perceptual pick-up, a more intense alertness to detail especially at near distance, and a more decisive and delimited attention to visual tasks. Contrariwise, children with highly developed peripheral vision show a more deliberate initial pick-up, a wider awareness of contexts, and a more marginal and circumspect approach to a visual situation. Comparable and correlated characteristics show themselves in other situations, social, adaptive, and communicative. Focal behavior tends to be forthright and sharply directed toward targets and objectives. Peripheral behavior is relatively cautious and tentative. Life makes demands on both kinds of behavior and the most balanced individuals are those who can modulate between dual alternatives and keep them within reciprocal control. Given a basic temperament and neuromotor equipment, the emotionally well-balanced child is also one who can modulate to a reasonable degree between dual alternatives. Emotions are tightly linked with motor attitudes and counterpoised tensions.

The child's development is beset with dualities both intrinsic and extrinsic. The wisdom of the body takes care of many of his most interior dualities; the wisdom of the culture must help him with others. Children vary enormously with respect to their capacity to adjust to internal and external stress. Certain kinds of stress are normal and necessary to the growth process. Such stresses are in fact created by the organism and may be regarded as developmental forces. Happy the child who has the potential and the opportunity to resolve resultant tensions and conflicts.

A tight-rope walker maintains a balance by leaning first left then right then left in rapid reciprocation. He returns toward a golden mean after each shift, and this enables him to step forward even though he fluctuates from side to side. He brings flexors and extensors into repeated counterpoise; he modulates his movements. If he is unable to modulate, he cannot walk a rope or even a plank. This simple analysis illustrates the basic mechanism of motor control and also affords a hint as to the growth of higher forms of self-control. Both forms of control are developmentally subject to the far-reaching principle of reciprocal interweaving.

In the acquisition of sphincter-bladder control the child at one stage may overhold and at another stage he may overrelease. Only with greater maturity and with diminishing fluctuations between these two extremes does he bring his sphincter functions under smoother modulated control. Naturally children display deep-seated individual differences in the manner in which they bring all their self-controls to increasing effectiveness. These are developmental differences which influence not only single episodes of behavior but the longer reach and the epochs of the life cycle. Every child reveals himself in a growth pattern which is the master key to his individuality.

This brief survey of the sources and manifestations of individuality indicates the importance of a developmental frame of reference. To fully understand a child we must think of him in terms of his growth characteristics. Single episodes of behavior may be very revealing; they are most revealing when interpreted in the perspective of the growth cycle. There is a developmental principle of relativity which applies to all forms of observation of child behavior. It applies with special force in the responsible realm of clinical observation. The concluding chapters therefore are concerned with the clinical protection of child development, and the cultural implications of a developmental philosophy of child care.

CHAPTER EIGHT

The Diagnosis and Supervision
of Development

Methods of Behavior Examination and Clinical Applications

Development as well as disease falls within the scope of clinical medicine. This is pre-eminently true of pediatrics which is virtually a form of general medicine responsible for the protection of early human growth. The general practitioner in his capacity as child and family physician, the child neurologist, and child psychiatrist also are concerned with the diagnosis and supervision of development.

Development is an inclusive, integrative concept which embraces the "total health" of a growing organism. The concept applies with equal force to the well child and to the handicapped. It applies conjointly to physical and to mental health. In fact, child health may be defined as that condition which permits and promotes optimal development.

Development makes itself manifest in three different kinds of signs and symptoms: anatomic, physiologic, and behavioral. These are all interrelated, but behavior is the most comprehensive index of an infant's maturity and well-being. Behavior assumes patterns which change with increasing maturity and which can be objectively examined. Developmental diagnosis is an appraisal of maturity status, and is largely based on graded functional tests of behavior to determine the maturity and the integrity of the action system. Such tests are significant for all types of children, normal as well as defective and handicapped.

It is noteworthy that over half of the professional time of the pediatrician is devoted to well children. A recent public statement of the American Board of Pediatrics recommends "the teaching of physical, mental, emotional and social growth in their interrelationship, since one of the most important functions of the pediatrician is the guidance of the total growth, development and ultimate social adjustment of the individual." The medical protection of the infant begins with the regulation of nutrition and with preventive immunization, but a broader protection must include mental as well as physical health. This can be accomplished by a developmental type of pediatrics, which utilizes clinical norms and methods to ascertain the achieved status and growth potentials of the infant and young child.

Such clinical protection of infant development involves a more systematic regard for behavior symptoms in private and group practice, in infant welfare conferences, in child-caring agencies, institutions, and hospitals. At a minimum there should be a behavior inventory which will register normal trends and disclose the more serious developmental defects and deviations. A simple screening behavior examination is feasible even under the conditions of a crowded practice.

As a clinical technique, developmental examinations may be undertaken at various levels of skill and thoroughness. As a diagnostic specialty, this technique requires postgraduate training and a diversified clinical experience with normal, atypical, and defective infants and young children.

Although the procedures of a behavior examination are simple in principle, their effectiveness depends upon the clinical judgment and acumen of the examiner. Because of his clinical experience he can use the behavior tests as controlled devices for eliciting patterns of behavior indicative of developmental status. Any developmental estimate, whether based on a brief inventory or on a formal examination, should be supplemented by an interview, a developmental history, and incidental observations. Four major fields of behavior must be taken into account as follows:

Motor behavior: posture and locomotion; prehension and manipulation; eye-hand co-ordination.

Adaptive behavior: self-initiated and induced behavior; learning, resourcefulness in adjusting to new situations, exploitive behavior.

Language behavior: vocalizations, gestures, vocal signs, words, comprehension.

Personal-social behavior: reactions to persons; responses to gesture, and child care; self-help.

A diagnostic appraisal considers each of the foregoing fields separately and does not attempt to express the degree of maturity in a single averaged numerical index, such as an I.Q. Developmental diagnosis is concerned with levels and patterns of maturity which must be formulated in interpretive statements, using specific age norms for descriptive clarity. When diagnoses are made of the same child at advancing ages, the results of successive examinations can be constructively compared with each other in an analytic manner.

In clinically experienced hands a developmental behavior examination, conducted formally and with precision of purpose, serves several functions as follows: (1) It ascertains stages of maturity in distinguishable fields of behavior; (2) It yields an analytic appraisal of normal, deviant, and defective aspects of the action system; (3) It may bring to early light otherwise unrecognized neurological impairments; (4) It sets up a life situation which renders objective information as to emotional stability, personality structure, and parent-child relationships; (5) Thereby it implements a periodic type of developmental supervision focused upon the interpretation and guidance of growth potentials, both in normal and in handicapped children.

How does a developmental examination correspond to a life situation? Without attempting to describe procedures in full, we can sketch in outline the course of events in the examination, say, of a twenty-eight-week-old infant referred for diagnosis. The observation of behavior begins the moment the child arrives at the clinic. How the child deploys his eyes and attention, how he and his mother react to each other may soon become evident. Incidental observations can be made during the preliminary interview, but we delay direct contact with the infant; we aim to disarm any distrust on his part. We do not begin the formalized examination until we have the infant's confidence. He watchfully makes his own observations while we are talking to his mother, and concludes that we have no aggressive designs upon him. After some minutes (the time is variable) he accepts a toy which we have been careful not to press upon him too early. His full acceptance of the toy is a token of adjustment and is a sign that the behavior examination in the clinical crib may begin.

We relate these details because they represent what may be called *a life situation technique*. The discerning infant demands a courteous amount of considerate approach before he enters into a transaction. And a behavior examination should be a two-way transaction in which examiner and infant co-operate to produce optimal reactions. Then the examination becomes part of a legitimate life situation from which to deduce diagnostic conclusions.

When the preliminary adjustments have been safeguarded, the infant typically addresses himself to the test materials with all the zeal and resources at his command. In fifteen minutes or less he puts forth a wealth of revealing behavior patterns, sensorimotor, adaptive, and interpersonal. Attentional and emotional traits are displayed in the manner in which he makes transitions from one test situation to another and in the manner in which he adjusts to the examination as a whole. The entire series of events from his arrival to his departure has been a life experience for him. The clinician makes a judicious estimate of how he, the infant, has met the experience. The mother who sat by during the examination has reacted to the experience in her own way. The father may have witnessed the examination from a one-way-vision observation room.

This degree of participation on the part of the parents becomes of special importance if the infant in question presents some handicap or difficulty which causes anxiety. The parents must feel that the child has had a careful, thorough examination by a conscientious and interested physician. All this helps the parents toward a better understanding of the child when problems are discussed in the conference which follows the examination. The task of the physician is to interpret the child and his growth potentials. Explanations of the mutually observed behavior elicited by the developmental examination facilitates mutual understanding. These advantages increase with each successive examination. Developmental diagnosis leads naturally into a developmental supervision, based on a series of progressively interrelated examinations.

Such follow-up supervision becomes of extreme importance whenever the physician, as pediatrician or general practitioner, is confronted by the parents of a handicapped infant. Above all else, the parents will wish to know what effect the handicap will have on the course of the child's development. The handicaps take many different forms—cerebral palsies, congenital anomalies, convulsive disorders, mental defects, retardation, endocrine abnormalities, sensory impairments, blindness, deafness, prematurity.* When the

* For a concrete discussion of these various types of handicap, the reader may consult the revised, enlarged edition of the basic clinical volume by Gesell & Amatruda, entitled DEVELOPMENTAL DIAGNOSIS: *Normal and Abnormal Child Development* (P. Hoeber, Inc., Medical Department of Harper & Brothers, New

child is handicapped by a parent with psychopathic personality and extremely abnormal attitudes, the physician will seek the aid of a psychiatric practitioner. But these instances are exceptional. Most parent guidance and family counseling deals with relatively normal and manageable aspects of parent-child and sibling relationships. Here the work of the pediatrician becomes highly personal. He functions as a family physician, a role which will become of increasing importance with the growing complexity of our culture and with the social applications of medical science.

It is sometimes feared that with impending changes in the financing of clinical health services, the personal bonds between physician and family will be broken. So far as the pediatrician is concerned, this is not a necessary consequence. He can insist that adequate protection of child health depends upon a personalized relationship with the family unit and upon an individualized consecutive form of developmental supervision progressively maintained from birth through infancy and childhood.

The problems of care and treatment are complex and require a high degree of co-operation on the part of all concerned. They call for some insight into the concrete effect of the handicap on the psychology of the child and on the mental growth processes. The initial guidance and orientation should come from the supervising physician. His advice and direction will depend upon his first developmental appraisal and his follow-up reappraisals. The problems of developmental handicap usually have a deep emotional setting which demands a high order of applied mental hygiene. The pediatrician and general practitioner have an important and inescapable role in protecting the welfare of the handicapped infant and preschool child.

But modern pediatrics is pre-eminently a form of preventive medicine. It holds the most strategic position in the whole scheme of public health. It is medically responsible for the welfare of the newborn infant and his continuing growth. It is concerned with the maintenance of normality and the constructive, positive aspects of health protection.

These are the social and cultural reasons why pediatric medicine

---

York, 1947; pp. 496). Separate chapters are devoted to the developmental symptoms and behavior traits of different forms of handicap and defect. Special attention is given to the neurological diagnosis of infant behavior by developmental methods. The procedures of developmental diagnosis are further illustrated in Appendix D. of the present volume.

may well assume a role of leadership in the conservation of mental health. In our American society the physician in his pediatric capacity is most intimately identified with family life, and as counselor he exercises a profound influence upon the standards and practices of child care. His influence will be far-reaching if he can function with clinical authority in a purposeful form of developmental supervision which is concerned with the psychologic aspects of well-being.

CHAPTER NINE

A Developmental Philosophy

Its Significance for Child Care and Mental Health

There are three major brands of philosophy which deal with the principles and practices of child care: (1) authoritarian; (2) laissez-faire; (3) developmental. The authoritarian approach insists on the priority of the culture. It also holds that children are habit-forming creatures, who should be molded to the patterns of the culture, through training, learning, and conditioned reflexes. Behaviorism as a social theory concedes little to the child's heredity and magnifies the influence vested in the environment. In its extreme form it leads to totalitarian trends of thought in home, school, and government.

Laissez-faire doctrine, on the contrary, imposes no constraint on the child or on the culture. Let things take their own wise course: the child will know and select what is best for him if he is not confused and restricted by unnatural requirements. This outlook leads to the policy of noninterference. It encourages great freedom of action for the child, and demands a corresponding indulgence on the part of the adult.

A developmental philosophy in temper and in principle lies between the two foregoing extremes. In matters of child care a developmental outlook is suspicious of authoritarian absolutes and it does not favor license. It is sensitive to the relativities of growth and is concerned with the changing needs of the child. A developmental philosophy acknowledges the profound forces of racial and familial inheritance which determine the growth sequences and the distinctive growth pattern of each individual child.

It is easy to see how these three contrastive and rival brands of philosophy affect all human relationships, especially those between adult and child. The conflicts in point of view have by no means been resolved. Many current ideas about child behavior are essentially pre-Darwinian in their absoluteness. The concept of evolution as it applies to the race is much more widely appreciated and accepted than the corollary concept of growth as it applies to infant and child. We still tend to approach the problems of child care, child discipline, and even of child education in terms of flat absolutes without awareness of the depth-dimension of development. Our culture at present is more rational about the physical universe than it is about children. The lawfulness of nuclear energy, of light and gravity, is freely granted. It is becoming apparent that the human life cycle is equally governed by natural laws.

In surety and precision the laws of development are comparable to those of gravitation. This fact gives ground for faith. It means that the remarkable advances of the life sciences and the physical sciences can ultimately lead to a greater comprehension and control of the forces of life and growth.

Meanwhile, a developmental philosophy favors a better understanding of the child, besieged as he is by a highly technological culture. This philosophy enables us to see the child as an ever-changing organism in a long but lawful cycle of growth. His behavior as a member of the species and as an individual thus takes on more meaning and truer proportions. His distinctive growth characteristics prove to be the essence of his individuality and by the same token a key to his educability.

The dynamics of development are by no means limited to the early embryology of behavior. Our studies have demonstrated that the higher psychical manifestations of the child life also are profoundly subject to the laws of development. Psychically, the child inherits nothing fully formed. Each and every part of his nature has to grow—his sense of self; his fears, his affections and his curiosities; his feelings toward mother, father, playmates, and sex; his judgments of good and bad, of ugly and beautiful; his respect for truth and property; his sense of humor; his ideas about life and death, crime, war, nature, and deity. All his sentiments, concepts, and attitudes are products of growth and experience. For all these diverse areas of behavior it is possible to formulate gradients of growth which represent the natural maturational stages by which the child assimilates the complex culture into which he is born.

He manifests his individuality from the very beginning in his natural rhythms of feeding, sleep, and self-activity. Given wisely managed opportunity, he seems to know when to sleep, when to be hungry, and how much to sleep and eat. His educability is not so bland and undifferentiated that he responds neatly to an iron-clad feeding schedule. Things work out better if his own self-regulation mechanisms, which are really growth mechanisms, are given a reasonable scope. The discerning physician makes no arbitrary distinctions between physical and mental factors; he gives conjoint consideration to the infant's nutritional status, to his immunities, allergies, and behavior traits. The child grows as a unit.

The task of the culture, likewise, is to watch for signs and symptoms of the child's total well-being with a special concern for psychological health. We must go along with the infant far enough to give him a sense of security. But self-dependence is fully as important. Step by step it is possible to build up his self-reliance and a self-confidence based upon confidence in his caretakers. Gradually he gains in morale and social insights, not through sheer indulgence, but through perceptive guidance on the part of his elders. And the more these elders know about the processes of growth, the more they will respect the truly remarkable progress which normal children make even in the first five years of life.

The intrinsic badness of children has been vastly exaggerated by distorting interpretations of their misbehavior. Well-constituted children with healthy inheritance have an intrinsic charm—a charm which betokens intrinsic goodness. The growth potentials for good far outweigh those for evil, unless the cultural odds are too heavily weighted against the child.

It is too freely said that science is indifferent to human values. Science by implication is always concerned with values, and the life sciences which deal with the physiology and the pathologies of growth are profoundly coming to grips with the deepmost determiners of human values. The race evolved; the child grows. And we shall not have the requisite self-knowledge to manage our culture until we make a more sedulous effort to understand the ways of all growth and the potentials of child growth, which are the culminating evidences and products of organic evolution.

This evolution has not ceased, and to that degree man still remains educable. He seems to have reached the very acme of mass cruelty, confusion, conflict, and destructiveness. Therein lies a tithe of hope. It would seem that on sheer evolutional grounds of survival, man must and can shift to a higher cerebral plane of attitude and action. Among other things he surely needs a science of behavior, a systematically prosecuted science, which will not only probe the lingering wickedness of Old Adam, but which will explore with unrelenting penetration the rich repository of potentials for good, which are revealed with awesome mystery in the sequences of child development.

APPENDIX A

GENERAL REFERENCES

Barcroft, Joseph. *The Brain and Its Environment*. New Haven: Yale University Press, 1938, XI, 117.

Cobb, Stanley. *A Preface to Nervous Disease*. Baltimore: Wood, 1936, VII, 173.

Cobb, Stanley. *Emotions and Clinical Medicine*. New York: 1950, p. 243.

Coghill, G. E. *Anatomy and the Problem of Behavior*. New York: Macmillan, 1929, XII, 113.

Corner, George W. *Ourselves Unborn. Natural History of the Human Embryo*. New Haven: Yale University Press, 1944.

Eulenburg-Wiener, Renee von. *Fearfully and Wonderfully Made. The Human Organism in the Light of Modern Science*. New York: Macmillan, 1938, XII, 472.

Hooker, Davenport. *Reflex Activities in the Human Fetus*. Chapter 2 in *Child Behavior and Development*. Edited by Roger G. Barker, Jacob S. Kounin, and Herbert F. Wright. New York and London: McGraw-Hill, 1943, VIII, 652.

Magnus, R. Korperstellung. Berlin: Springer, 1924, XIII, 740.

Needham, Joseph (F.R.S.F). *A History of Embryology*. Cambridge: University Press, 1934, XVIII, 274.

Preyer, W. *Specielle Physiologie des Embryo* (Leipzig, 1885). Trans. by George E. Coghill and Wolfram K. Legner: *Embryonic Motility and Sensitivity. Monograph of the Society for Research in Child Development*, 2, No. 6 (serial no. 13), p. 115.

Thompson, D'Arcy Wentworth. *On Growth and Form*. Cambridge: University Press, 1942, 1116 pp.

Windle, William Frederick. *Physiology of the Fetus: Origin and Extent of Function in Prenatal Life*. Philadelphia and London: W. B. Saunders, 1940, XIII, 249.

DEVELOPMENTAL DATA

The following publications report the basic investigations of the behavior norms and sequences of infant development, referred to in the present volume:

Gesell, A. *et al. An Atlas of Infant Behavior:* A systematic delineation of the forms and early growth of human behavior patterns, in two volumes, illustrated by 3,200 action photographs. New Haven: Yale University Press, 1934, Volume One: Normative Series, pp. 1-524; Volume Two: Naturalistic Series, pp. 525-922.

Gesell, A. and Thompson, H., assisted by Amatruda, C. S. *The Psychology of Early Growth* including Norms of Infant Behavior and a Method of Genetic Analysis. New York: Macmillan, 1938, IX, 290.

Gesell, A. and Thompson, H., assisted by Amatruda, C. S. *Infant Behavior: Its Genesis and Growth*. New York: McGraw-Hill, 1934, VIII, 343.

Gesell, A. in collaboration with Amatruda, C. S. *The Embryology of Behavior: The Beginnings of the Human Mind*. New York: Harper, 1945, pp. XIX, 289.

APPENDIX B

COLLATERAL READINGS

The publications listed below deal concretely with the procedures of developmental diagnosis, and also with problems of child and parent guidance from a developmental point of view.

The books which contain material most closely related to the present volume are indicated by an asterisk.

Gesell, A. and Ilg, F. L. *Feeding Behavior of Infants: A Pediatric Approach to the Mental Hygiene of Early Life.* Philadelphia: Lippincott, 1937, IX, 201.

An outline of the developmental neurology of feeding behavior patterns. Presents detailed clinical data on the reactions of infants reared on self-regulation schedules of feeding and sleep. Deals with the principles and management of self-regulatory procedures. Special sections on weaning, finger sucking, sphincter control, etc.

Aldrich, C. A., and M. M. *Babies Are Human Beings.* New York: Macmillan, 1938, 128.

A readable volume, which stresses the individuality of the infant and his growth needs.

Gesell, A. *et al. The First Five Years of Life. A Guide to the Study of the Preschool Child.* New York: Harper, 1940, XIII, 393.

A year-by-year account. Special chapters on the conduct and philosophy of developmental examination. Discusses clinical adaptations to atypical conditions.

* Gesell, A. and Ilg, F. L. *Infant and Child in the Culture of Today: The Guidance of Development.* New York: Harper, 1943, XII, 399.

A practical guidance book addressed to parents and child welfare workers. Will assist the physician in planning guidance measures for the periodic supervision of child development.

*Gesell, A., assisted by K. G. Walden. *How a Baby Grows: A Story in Pictures.* New York: Harper, 1945, VII, 78.

A picture story portraying the growth of infant behavior with 800 action photographs. A simple introduction to a development point of view.

*Gesell, A. in collaboration with Amatruda, C. S. *The Embryology of Behavior: The Beginnings of the Human Mind.* New York: Harper, 1945, pp. XIX, 289.

An ontogenetic account of the patterning of fetal and neonatal behavior from the standpoint of development morphology. Based on clinical and cinematic studies of fetal infants. Illustrated by over 300 action photographs.

Spock, Benjamin. *The Common Sense Book of Baby and Child Care.* New York: Duell, Sloan, and Pearce, 1945, 527.

This book is written with a direct, simple style. The author applies the principles of growth and development in his instructions to mothers.

Gesell, A. and Ilg, F. L. *The Child from Five to Ten.* New York: Harper, 1946, XII, 475.

A companion volume to *Infant and Child in the Culture of Today.* Growth gradients and guidance suggestions in ten major fields of behavior: motor characteristics, personal hygiene, emotional expression, fears and dreams, self and sex, interpersonal relations, play and pastimes, school life, ethical sense, philosophic outlook.

*Gesell, A. and Amatruda, C. S., *Developmental Diagnosis: Normal and Abnormal Child Development.* New York: Hoeber, 1947 (2nd Edition), XVI, 496.

A clinical manual describing in detail, the procedures of developmental examination and the behavior development of normal infants. Behavior patterns and growth trends characteristic of each age level from four weeks to three years are delineated and illustrated by over one hundred photo tracings. Clinical behavior, studies of amentia, endocrine disorders, convulsive disorders, brain injuries, blindness, deafness, prematurity, precocity, environmental retardation, child adoption.

McQuarrie, Irivine. *Brennemann's Practice of Pediatrics.* Hagerstown: Prior, 1948, 4 volumes in loose leaf.

This standard work includes several chapters which deal directly with developmental aspects of therapy, guidance, and health supervision:

> Washburn, Alfred H.: "The Appraisal of Healthy Growth and Development from Birth to Adolescence."
>
> Wetzel, N. C.: "Measurement of Physical Growth." (Analysis of trends with the aid of a growth grid.)
>
> Gessell, A. "Developmental Diagnosis and Supervision."
>
> Richards, E. L.: "Mental Hygiene."
>
> Brennemann, Joseph: "Examination of the Child."

Gesell, A. *Studies in Child Development.* New York: Harper, 1948, X, 224.

Essays and addresses dealing with child development as a clinical and a social science. Chapters on genius, giftedness, and growth; the method of co-twin control; the predictiveness of infant behavior.

* Gesell, A., Ilg, F. L., Bullis, G. E. *Vision: Its Development in Infant and Child.* New York: Hoeber, 1949, XVI, 329.

Traces the normal growth of visual functions from birth to ten years. Relates visual behavior patterns to the ontogenesis of the total action system. Special sections deal with the hygiene of child vision and the developmental aspects of visual defects.

APPENDIX C

The Photographic Research Library of the Yale Films of Child Development consists of the intact original cinema records of the behavior patterning of normal and of clinically deviant infants and children. These extensive active records have been catalogued and analytically indexed for convenient teaching and research reference.

Edited sequences in sound and silent versions have been organized and are available through Encyclopedia Britannica Films, Inc., Research and Production Departments, 1150 Wilmette Avenue, Wilmette, Illinois. The sound films carry a spoken commentary (by Gesell) and are designed to give a systematic view of the course of normal child development.

Sound Series. The subject matter of these individual sound films (each 400 feet in length in 16 mm. size) is indicated by the following titles:

(1) *The Growth of Infant Behavior: Early Stages*
Behavior of infant at 8, 12, 16, and 20 weeks of age. Animated diagrams to illustrate the concept of behavior patterns.

(2) *The Growth of Infant Behavior: Later Stages*
Animated diagrams depicting the growth of the fetal hand. The patterning of cube behavior at 24, 28, 40, and 52 weeks, portrayed by coincident projection of adjacent ages.

(3) *Posture and Locomotion*
Typical postural behavior at 13 successive age levels.

(4) *From Creeping to Walking*
Creeping, cruising, pivoting, assisted and independent walking.

(5) *A Baby's Day at 12 Weeks*
Record of a total behavior day, showing child care situations: sleep, bath, feeding, sunning, etc.

(6) *A Thirty-Six Weeks Behavior Day*
A similar record of the same infant six months later, showing progress in performance and social maturity.

(7) *A Behavior Day at Forty-Eight Weeks*
The cycle of a representative domestic day. Psychological aspects of child care in the home.

(8) *Behavior at One Year*
Characteristic behavior patterns as demonstrated by reactions to developmental test situations.

(9) *Learning and Growth*
Comparative delineations of the same child at different ages to show the dependence of learning ability on maturity factors.

(10) *Early Social Behavior*
Ten children from eight weeks to seven years of age are depicted in a variety of social situations to reveal individual and maturity differences.

The foregoing films are relatively nontechnical in character, and were designed for group instruction rather than individual study. They outline the course of normal development in sufficient detail to serve as a background for the more technical use.

Silent Series. The subject matter of the individual silent films (each 400 feet in length, 16 mm. size) is indicated by the following titles:

(1) *How Behavior Grows: The Patterning of Prone Progression*
This film traces stage by stage the manner in which a baby acquires the power to creep and to rise from a horizontal to an upright position.

(2) *The Growth of Motor Behavior in the First Five Years of Life*
Deals chiefly with the finer motor co-ordinations and discriminations which the mind makes in its conquest of the world of things. This world is here typified by test cubes, pellet, and paper and pencil.

(4) *Infants Are Individuals: The Beginnings of Personality*
Motor, adaptive, and personal-social behaviors of several children are depicted in such a way as to show that each individual has a distinctive behavior make-up which manifests itself in infancy as well as in later life.

(5) *Twins Are Individuals: Twins T and C from Infancy to Adolescence*
Cross sections of the behavior of these twins from infancy through adolescence disclose not only striking similarities but also consistent differences which continue into the teens.

(6) *The Baby's Bath*
Depicts the baby's bath at varying ages in homelike surroundings. Calls attention to the behavior aspects of the bath experiences.

(7) *Bottle and Cup Feeding*
Delineates guidance suggestions. The progressive motor co-ordinations displayed in the bottle and cup-feeding situations at advancing age levels.

(8) *The Conquest of the Spoon*
A similar developmental portrayal of the mastery of the spoon as a complicated cultural tool.

(9) *Self-discovery in a Mirror*
The baby's reaction to his mirror image reflects the advancing stages in the organization of his social behavior.

(10) *Early Play*
Portrays both spontaneous and induced play activities at advancing stages of maturity.

The research methods and diagnostic and guidance service of the former Yale Clinic of Child Development were recorded in 1946 in a documentary film produced by *March of Time*, 369 Lexington Avenue, New York City. This film is available as an educational film in the Forum edition. The current activities of the Gesell Institute of Child Development were recently documented for television broadcast in *The March of Time over the Years* series (1951).

APPENDIX D

ILLUSTRATIONS OF PRINCIPLES AND METHODS OF DEVELOPMENTAL DIAGNOSIS AT 28 WEEKS LEVEL OF MATURITY

Adapted from Gesell and Amatruda Manual on Developmental Diagnosis, *published by Hoeber, N. Y. This manual covers 24 ages from 4 weeks through 3 years.*

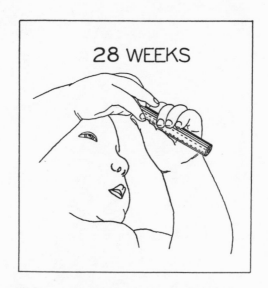

There are eight key ages from four weeks to three years corresponding to four developmental periods or maturity zones:

KEY AGES	MATURITY ZONE
4 weeks)	Supine
16 weeks)	
28 weeks)	Sitting
40 weeks)	
12 months)	Locomotor
18 months)	
24 months)	
36 months)	Preschool
48 months)	
60 months)	

For illustrative purposes the twenty-eight weeks level is outlined in the following manner:

(1) Action drawings portray characteristic behavior patterns (pages 96-97).
(2) The associated text gives a condensed narrative picture of the developmental examination and of typical behavior. The text specifies (in italics) all behavior which characteristically appears for the first time at each key age (pages 97-98).
(3) A developmental schedule codifies the behavior patterns for diagnostic application (page 99).
(4) Finally a summary of growth trends delineates the drift of the developing behavior (pages 100-102).

Additional maturity traits and trends are suggested in terms of Feeding Behavior, Visual Behavior, and Behavior Day.

1. Holds cubes more than momentarily

5. Transfers and mouths bell

2. Transfers cube

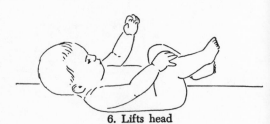

6. Lifts head

3. Rakes at pellet

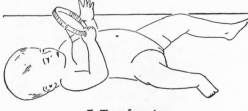

7. Transfers ring

4. Bangs bell

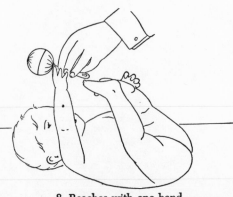

8. Reaches with one hand

(1)

9. Sits momentarily leaning on hands

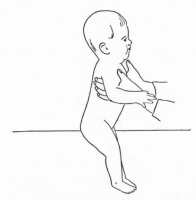

10. Sustains large fraction of weight; bounces

11. Regards image; pats glass

12. Feet to mouth

(2)   TWENTY-EIGHT WEEKS

The 28-week-old infant sits with support, his trunk erect and head steady. After a brief period with an introductory toy, it is removed and the examiner presents the FIRST of three CUBES. The baby seizes it *immediately* with a *radial palmar* grasp and carries it to his mouth. He *retains* it as the SECOND CUBE is presented. He does not grasp the second cube but he holds 2 *cubes more than momentarily* (1) when they are placed in his hands. As the THIRD CUBE is presented, he drops a cube. He does not grasp the third cube but mouths, *transfers* (2), drops and resecures the cube in hand.

He follows the screen as it is removed from the MASSED CUBES, then approaches the mass with both hands, grasping one cube and scattering the others. *Holding one cube he grasps another;* he may pick up 3 in all.

He follows the examiner's hand away as the PELLET is presented; gives delayed, intent regard to the pellet, and *rakes* (3) at it with his fingers, *contacting it.*

He makes an *immediate one-handed* approach on the BELL, taking it by the bowl or junction. He *bangs* (4), mouths and *transfers* (5) the bell, *retaining* it without dropping.

The RING AND STRING are presented, the string obliquely aligned to the right, but within reach. He *reaches toward the ring,* slaps and scratches the table, and finally sees the string; he either *abandons the effort or fusses.*

The test table is removed. He is placed on his back on the platform. His SUPINE posturings are symmetrical, with the legs lifted high in extension or semi-extension. He *lifts the head* (6) as though striving to sit up. He is none too tolerant of the supine position and this and the following three situations may have to be curtailed or omitted.

He grasps, *transfers* (7) and mouths the DANGLING RING, regarding it in hand.

He makes an *immediate one-handed approach* (8) upon the RATTLE, *shakes* it vigorously, regards it and fingers it with the free hand. If it is placed on the platform at his side, he reaches for it unsuccessfully.

When auditory responses are tested by RINGING A BELL opposite first one ear, then the other, he turns his head correctly and promptly.

The examiner now takes his hands and he lifts his head and assists in the PULL-TO-SITTING. In the SITTING position he *sits for a moment, leaning forward, propped* on his hands (9). He also shows some *active balance, sitting erect for a fleeting, unsteady moment.*

Held in the STANDING position, he sustains a *large fraction of weight* (10) on his extended legs as he *bounces* actively.

Placed PRONE, he holds the head well lifted, his weight on his abdomen and hands. He *lifts one arm* toward a lure and he *tries, unsuccessfully, to pivot.*

Seated before a MIRROR, he regards his image, smiles, vocalizes and *pats the glass* (11).

His LANGUAGE includes cooing, squealing, and *combined vowel sounds.* He says *m-m-mum* when he cries.

His mother REPORTS that he discriminates strangers, "talks" to his toys, *takes solids well,* and even *brings his feet to his mouth* (12). He rolls from supine to prone and sits propped about half an hour.

Normative Behavior characteristic of the KEY AGE: 28 WEEKS and adjacent age levels is codified by the *Developmental Schedules* shown on the following page.

(3) DEVELOPMENTAL SCHEDULES OF NORMATIVE ITEMS

KEY AGE: 28 Weeks

24 Weeks	28 Weeks	32 Weeks
Motor		
Su: lifts legs high in ext.	Su: lifts head (*40w)	Sit: 1 min., erect, unsteady (*36w)
Su: rolls to prone	Sit: briefly, leans fwd. (on hands) (*32w)	St: maintains briefly, hands held (*36w)
P. Sit: lifts head, assists (*40w)	Sit: erect momentarily	Pr: pivots (*40w)
Sit. chair: trunk erect (*36w)	St: large fraction of weight (*36w)	Pellet: radial raking (*36w)
Cube: grasps, palmarwise (*36w)	St: bounces actively (*32w)	Pellet: unsuccessful inferior scissors (*36w)
Ra: retains	Cube: radial palmar grasp (*36w)	
	Pellet: rakes (whole hand), contacts(*32w)	
Adaptive		
D. Ring, Ra, Cube, Bell: approaches & grasps	Ra, Bell: 1 hand approach & grasp	Cube: grasps 2nd cube
Ra: prehen. pursuit dropt Ra	M. Cubes: holds 1, grasps another	Cube: retains 2 as 3rd presented
Cube: regards 3rd cube immediately	Cube: holds 2 more than momentarily	Cube: holds 2 prolongedly
Cube, Bell: to mouth (*18m)	Bell: bangs (*40w)	Cup-cu: holds cube, regards cup
Cube: resecures dropt cube	Ra: shakes definitely	Ring-str: secures ring
M. Cubes: holds 1, approaches another	D. Ring, Cube: transfers	
	Bell: transfers adeptly	
	Bell: retains	
Language		
Bell-r: turns head to bell	Vo: m-m-m (crying) (*40w)	Vo: single syllable as da, ba, ka
Vo: grunts, growls (*36w)	Vo: polysyllabic vowel sounds (*36w)	
Vo: spontan. vocal-social (incl. toys)		
Personal-Social		
So: discriminates strangers	Feeding: takes solids well	Play: bites, chews toys (*18m)
Play: grasps foot (supine) (*36w)	Play: with feet to mouth (supine) (*36w)	Play: reaches persistently for toys out of reach (*40w)
Play: sits propped 30 min. (*40w)	Mirror: reaches, pats image	Ring-str: persistent
Mirror: smiles and vocalizes	Ring-str: fusses or abandons effort (*32w)	

(4)   Growth Trends

One of the major goals of infant development is the upright posture. The 28-week-old infant is chronologically and developmentally at a half-way station on the road to this goal. He is just beginning to sit alone, erecting his trunk for a brief moment. After he has doubled his age, at 56 weeks, he stands alone.

When the 28-week infant is placed supine, he manifests this urge to sit by lifting his head from the platform. This is a deeply ingrained propensity. Placed in a standing position, steadied by the trunk, his legs sustain a large fraction of weight. His arm control is, however, far in advance of his leg control. When securely placed in the examining chair he delights in exercising his new powers of manipulation. At 16 weeks he sat in rather stiff bilateral symmetry. Now his trunk is more supple, and he can make an eager unilateral forward thrust to reach an object like the hand bell. He is more mobile at shoulder, elbow and wrist joints. He is transcending the earlier phase of bilateral symmetry. Not only does he make a one-handed approach upon the bell, he shifts the bell from one hand to the other with startling adeptness.

This shuttle-like transfer has both symmetric and asymmetric features. Nature is weaving a very complicated neuro-motor fabric, laying down the warp and woof for that specialized functional asymmetry which goes by the everyday name of right-handedness or left-handedness. The 16-week infant is bidextrous; the 40-week infant will be unidextrous; the 28-week infant is bi-uni-dextrous. Hence his propensity for transfer and retransfer and retransfer again. It is one of his most typical patterns.

This same alternating type of action in the 32-week infant produces a circular translocation when he is placed on his stomach. Being geared to alternating movements, he flexes and extends his arms in successional turns, causing his trunk to pivot. (At a later age when his arms are again for a time geared to bilateral movements in the prone position, he pushes himself backward or drags himself forward.) At present his legs are not sufficiently developed for creeping.

The 28-week infant is therefore far in advance of the 16-week infant in patterns of prehension and his eyes continue to be more skillful than his fingers. Thanks to his ocular adjustments he can pick up a string perceptually; but he is very inept at plucking it with his fingers. Likewise he can give consistent (ocular) regard to a pellet; but he places his hand rather crudely over it and usually fails to secure it. Prompt precise prehension of the pellet comes at about 40 weeks, due to the specialization of the radial digits, thumb and forefinger. This too is a sort of functional asymmetry, based on developmental individuation. Interestingly enough, this more advanced asymmetry is already foreshadowed at 28 weeks. Even though the 28-week infant seizes the cube with a hand grasp rather than a finger grasp, he appropriates with the *radial* side of the hand. This *radial* palmar grasp foretells thumb opposition. As so often happens, a present behavior pattern is charged with implications for the future. Only rarely does a baby's behavior hark back to the past.

Although eyes are still in the lead, eyes and hands function in close interaction, each reinforcing and guiding the other. Whereas the 16-week-old infant is given to inspection of surroundings, the 28-week-old infant inspects objects. And if the object is within reach it is usually in his busy hands. Head became versatile in the previous trimester; hands became versatile in this one. As soon as he sees a cube he grasps it, senses surface and edges as he clutches it, brings it to his mouth, where he feels its qualities anew, withdraws it, looks at it on withdrawal, rotates it while he looks, looks while he rotates it, restores it to his mouth, withdraws it again for inspection, restores it again for mouthing, transfers it to the other hand, bangs it, contacts it with the free hand, retransfers, mouths it again, drops it, resecures it, mouths it yet again, repeating the cycle with variations— all in the time it takes to read this sentence.

The perceptual-manipulatory behavior of the 28-week-old infant is highly active. It is not passive reception. It is dynamic adaptivity, fused with exploitativeness. If you wish, it is intelligence.

His vocal behavior is filled with forward reference. It serves little immediate sociological purpose, but it does serve a neurological one. For in his diversified spontaneous vocalizations he is producing vowels, consonants, and even syllables and diphthongs, which in due time will eventuate in articulate communication. Even now an *m-m-m* utterance emerges when he cries.

Although he is verbally inarticulate, he is socially pretty wise. He knows what is going on around the house. He expresses eagerness and impatience as he sees his mother preparing food for him. He shows familiarity and anticipation in the routines of the household.

He recognizes strangers and tolerates them if they do not disappoint his expectancies. He is self-contained and will play for considerable periods by himself. Long ago he abandoned the hand play characteristic of 16 weeks. He plays with his feet instead, which represents at least a cephalo-caudad advance, and is part of his process of self-discovery. He is self-contained, content with his own devices. His very self-sufficiency makes him seem a more or less finished product. But in time he will make a clearer distinction between himself as a person and other persons. He is, in fact, laying the foundations for this more socialized perceptiveness.

ADDITIONAL TRAITS AND INDICATORS OF 28 WEEKS MATURITY LEVEL

4. FEEDING BEHAVIOR

Recognizes preliminaries of feeding.
Vocalizes eagerness on sight of bottle.
Manifests impatience until nipple is in mouth.
Purses lips expectantly on *presentation* of bottle.
Reaches forward with head.
Shows improved co-ordination of tongue and lips *during feeding*.
> Sucks continuously, with lower lip rolled out, and with pursing at corners. Less interference from tongue protrusion.
> Smacks or presses tongue against palate.
> Increased contraction of cheeks.
> Manages solids with less choking.
> Removes food from spoon with quick lip action.
Registers *satiety*.
> By straining toward a sitting posture, by smiling, by increased activity of hands.
> May express refusal by turning head to side and tightening lip closure.

5. VISUAL BEHAVIOR

When *supine*, lifts head and strains to sit up and inspect surroundings.
In supine self-activity brings feet into plane of vision for regard and manipulatory play.
> Also watches self-induced hand movements in manual play.
While supine, promptly regards and seizes dangling ring.
Looks discriminatingly at string from which ring is dangled. Resecures dropped ring.
When *sitting*, approaches string attached to ring on table surface.
> Regards handle of cup.
> Shifts in rapid alternation from grasp (of cube) to mouthing, to withdrawal, to swift regard on withdrawal, to manipulation, transfer, etc.
Moves eyes conjugately to explore contours of objects. Uses thumb in mesial opposition.
Increases radius of near regard and manipulation by extending arms forward to full length.

6. SPECIMEN BEHAVIOR DAY

Relative Time

6 to 8 A.M.	Awakes (usually soaking wet). Plays by self contentedly for 20 to 80 minutes (supine). Announces first self-demand for feeding.
7 A.M.	Propped in crib for play with toys and to watch activities of household.
9 A.M.	Fed in chair or on lap. (Bowel movement may occur after this feeding.)
10 A.M.	Naps in carriage or crib on porch.
12 P.M.–1 P.M.	Wakes. Plays contentedly for short period while supine and later while propped.
2 P.M.	Vegetable meal and breast or bottle feeding.
3 P.M.	Enjoys ride in carriage.
3:30 P.M.	Naps for about an hour.
4:30 P.M.	Orange juice and social play.
5 P.M.	Bath.
5:30 P.M.	Feeding.
6 P.M.	Asleep. Sleeps around the clock.

The foregoing lists of maturity traits and developmental indicators are suggestive and need not be applied too vigorously. With the kind of clinical caution which comes only from ordered experience, these and similar criteria assume orientational and diagnostic values in the appraisal of normality, subnormality, and abnormal deviation.

INDEX